SURVIVING YOUR CAREER

A Roadmap To Guide You During Your Career

Steven A. Sakofsky
Author and Consultant

Published 2010

Acknowledgement

This book was written during my working years and is based upon interactions with co-workers, supervisors and the operating philosophies of many organizations. I'm grateful to all of these people and organizations for their contribution for the content of the book.

I want to thank Jeanne Rashap for editing the book. Jeanne is a talented writer and editor who helped with organizing the content and attacking my grammar in order to develop coherent sentences.

Finally, my family contributed to the content since they had to put up with my job changes, relocations, travel, and long periods of time away from home.

Table to Contents

Chapter I – Introduction 6
   A. Hit the Ground Running 9
      1. Your first day 9
      2. Getting the "stuff" you need 16
      3. Your workspace 18
      4. Choosing your rabbi 20

Chapter II – Basic Survival Skills 23
   A. Surviving a Financial Crisis 23

   B. Need to Know 23
      1. Ethics 23
      2. Sick and personal days 28
      3. Religion and politics 30
      4. E-mail, internet and telephone 33
      5. Raising money in the office 36
      6. Gambling and office pools 38
      7. Drugs, alcohol and cigarettes 39
      8. Sex and the office 40

   B. Getting Along 41
      1. Cooperation is the key 41
      2. Office politics 44
      3. Bureaucratic nonsense 46
      4. Dealing with stupid people 48
      5. Trusting co-workers 50
      6. Losing your temper 52
      7. Overachieving 53
      8. Bored-looking busy 57

Chapter III – Getting the Job Done........................... 60
   A. Day In the Life... 60

      1. Completing tasks.................................. 60
      2. Meetings... 62
      3. Written communication......................... 65
      4. Monthly reports.................................... 67
      5. Giving presentations............................. 70
      6. Making mistakes.................................. 73
      7. Safety... 74

   B. You and Your Organization.......................... 77

      1. Who are the customers?....................... 77
      2. Quality and you.................................... 80
      3. Embrace the next big initiative................ 84
      4. Consultants... 86
      5. Business travel and entertaining.............. 91
      6. Company social events......................... 96
      7. Company sports teams......................... 99

   C. Tending Your Career................................. 100

      1. Your resume...................................... 100
      2. Training... 101
      3. Professional societies and certifications..... 107
      4. Performance evaluations..................... 110
      5. Compensation and how to get more of it... 113

Chapter IV – Considering Change 116

A. Within Your Current Organization 116

1. Moving to another city 116
2. Taking a job outside the United States 121
3. Your family's impact on your career 125
4. Exploring other options 128
5. Temporary assignments 131

B. Thinking About Leaving 133

1. When is it time to leave? 133
2. Job-hopping 139
3. Are you the oldest person left in the Organization? 141
4. How to quit 143
5. Gosh, I was fired or laid off 146
6. Headhunters 150
7. Networking 152

D. Other Options 153

1. Should you marry the boss' offspring 153
2. Working in a family-owned business 155
3. Starting your own business 157
4. Holding a second job or moonlighting 158

Chapter V – Conclusion 161

A. Managing Success and Survival 161
B. It's up to you 164
C. The Rules 164

CHAPTER I INTRODUCTION

Perhaps your father worked for the same company his entire career, climbed the organizational ladder, and retired with a decent pension and good benefits. Granted, it is probably more challenging for us to survive our careers today than it was for our parents—after all, this is a different day and time. But although you'll have to face risks, many unknowns, and certainly many situations beyond your control, you can achieve this same feat!

Throughout my career, I worked in the manufacturing side of various industrial product businesses, mainly in Quality Assurance/Control functions. I was an individual contributor, supervisor, manager, and a director responsible for the Quality function of a $500 million business. Some employers were giants with sales in the billions, but some were smaller businesses with sales in the $20 million range. During my career I received promotions, recognition for excellent work, and was laid off twice. In many of these positions, I was asked to hire people, but also had to fire people because of their performance or because business conditions were poor. So, after working in industry for 41 years, I find myself reflecting on my career.

Surviving Your Career

I survived my career, but I experienced both gratifying successes and serious wounds along the way. Difficulties and setbacks affected my progress: there were periods of unemployment, times when I had to live away from my family because of job changes, economic downturns, international upheavals, sale of companies, and personal health issues. However, opportunities and personal triumphs also propelled me forward. I became involved with quality system auditing as an instructor. I also worked with a National certification organization to assist in the development of processes for managing quality system auditor qualifications and qualifying organizations that sell Quality Management System certification to businesses.

I attribute my successes primarily to working hard and being in the right place at the right time. However, it's possible that if I had known the rules ahead of time, sought advice, and had a better roadmap, I would have had more successes and some of the wounds may have been avoided. When all was said and done, I concluded my professional career with dignity, a solid plan for a secure retirement, and no bitterness for any part of the 41 years of my professional life. I survived.

This book will work like a roadmap to help guide you along a number of different routes you can take in your career path. In many cases, you'll find advice that will require you to make choices. I also will give you some rules to follow. Regardless of your career choice or the type of organization you choose to join, these rules will always apply. If you remember anything from this book, remember the rules.

A. HIT THE GROUND RUNNING

Very simply, the process of interviewing for a job is a necessary game: One party—the interviewer—is attempting, to the best of his or her ability, to identify someone who has the qualifications to fill a position. The second party—the interviewee—is doing his or her best to convince the interviewer that he or she is fully qualified. To say the least, the hiring process is high drama!

1. YOUR FIRST DAY

Whatever the circumstance, once you have been through the interview process and accepted a position, it's crucial to start out on the right foot. Whether you are beginning your very first job or you are changing to a new job, sooner or later you'll be facing your first day on the job.

Location, location, location

Be sure you know the name of the person to whom you are to report, as well as the place you need to be to start the first day. Are you supposed to go to the Human Resources office? Are you supposed to arrive at the front door of the business? Is someone going to meet you and escort you to a designated office? Are you expected to find your own way to your workstation? It may be helpful to request that someone meet you at the front entrance and escort you to your starting point.

> **Rule # 1 Come in before your boss and leave after your boss leaves.**

Be on time and dress appropriately

A big part of these first steps is making a good impression. If you noted the "uniform of the day" during your interview process, you'll be able to select the appropriate clothing for your position. This is particularly important if your position requires safety protection. Ask about the safety requirements for dress and equipment before you start your new job or you may not be able to work on your first day. In many factories, basic safety equipment includes safety glasses and shoes. Safety glasses usually can be picked up at the door of a factory, but you may be expected to wear your own pair of safety shoes.

The paperwork

Come prepared with your own pen and notepad. Expect to fill out and sign a number of forms for taxes, health insurance, confidentiality statements, business security forms, life insurance forms, etc. Ask for explanations if you are not certain what these documents mean. If you do not understand what you are signing—don't sign. Your company may provide an employee orientation presentation with information related to company history, mission, the code of conduct, or safety guidelines. Request copies of these materials to refer to later if think you'll have trouble remembering some of the important details.

Making contact

During the first few days in a new position, you will be meeting new people and will probably encounter some you already met during the interview phase. Remember to smile, shake hands, maintain eye contact, answer questions, and try to remember names.

Most people have a terrible problem remembering people's names. There are several ways for improving your chances of remembering faces and names. First, use technology. If you ask permission first, you can use your cell phone to take a photo of a person you have met and then enter a text note of his or her name and position. Another method is to make your own "memory jogger." Ask for an organization chart and as you meet people, write a note next to a person's name that will help you remember, such as, "Tall brunette with glasses—35 years old." Finally, it's always appropriate to ask for a business card then make similar notes on the back.

Remember, this is not the time to crack jokes, nor is it the time to be aloof. Your success in this organization will depend on your ability to cooperate with others, so use this as your first opportunity to start to win friends and avoid making enemies.

The nuts and bolts

When you have found your workspace:

- Begin developing a list of the items you will need to do your job. Don't sweat the small stuff such as a stapler—focus on the critical items (e.g., furniture, electronics, etc.) and discuss any deficiencies with your supervisor. This also is a good opportunity to be resourceful: If the office space does not have a desk chair, put that on your list, then borrow any chair from a co-worker nearby so you can begin to work.
- Find the location of the restroom, copier, coffee, your supervisor's office, and those other staff members whose help you may need, such as an administrative assistant or secretary.
- Determine how to use the telephone, voice mail, and e-mail systems, and learn the proper protocol for answering the phone.
- Find out if time sheets are required, how often will you get paid, and in what form, such as a check, direct deposit, and so on.

You can probably learn other basic information through casual conversations with other co-workers: where you should park your vehicle; proper entry and exit procedures before and after normal business hours; process for emergency exit; location of the light switches for the office; location and hours for the cafeteria; company policy for using the office refrigerator; regulations about playing personal music; and how and where to get stationery supplies.

Your first meeting with your supervisor

As soon as you are settled, it's time for that first discussion with your supervisor about duties and expectations.

> **Rule # 2 The boss is always right.**

Look at it this way: In your work environment, your boss controls your destiny. If this person says the moon is made of cheese, simply ask, "What flavor?"

Your body language sends important messages about who you are and you're level of confidence. When you are sitting with your supervisor, speak distinctly and confidently, listen before you respond, and feel free to take a few notes. Be sure to make eye contact and do not slouch. Look for opportunities to inquire about how business is conducted within your new organization. If your supervisor does not raise the issue of a company orientation and the Human Resources department did not provide one, it's a good idea to ask if one is planned and how extensive it will be. Finally, determine how often you can expect a formal review of your performance.

Assignments

Asking who, what, where, and when will help ensure your success right from the start:

- Who is the lead person on the project? To whom should I report?
- What am I expected to deliver or accomplish?
- Where should I begin? Where can I find relevant materials?
- When should I begin the project?
- When is it due?

If you will be expected to produce periodic reports of your activities or output, it may be helpful to ask to see an example from one of your peers. (There will be a discussion of the content of activity reports later.)

Time to hold back

Here's a list of things that are not appropriate to ask for at this point:

- Time off within the next 6 months, unless it was agreed upon during the interview process.
- Special work hours.
- A better office location. More than likely, you are the low person on the totem pole and you'll get what is available.
- How soon you can expect a raise or a promotion. You have not done anything yet to merit this discussion.
- Additional responsibilities to the duties of your job when you interviewed. You are starting at a new position with its own set of objectives. The time to ask for additional responsibility will be after you have mastered all required tasks and are performing beyond acceptable expectations. In other words, don't try to be a hero too early without knowing if you can deliver on the original expectations.

Before you go home at the end of your first day, make some notes about what you have learned; the people you have met and what they do; questions you have based on what you have seen and heard; and an inventory of the items and equipment you need to do your job effectively.

2. GETTING THE "STUFF" YOU NEED

For now, "stuff" refers to anything you need to perform your job—stuff the company supplies and stuff you should provide. Ask your co-workers to help you understand this distinction.

The way to stuff

Most companies do not provide calculators to engineers. Why? Most engineers working today have their own calculators. Nurses probably have their own scissors. Machinists in many machine shops are required to bring their own measuring instruments. However, most organizations supply computers.

Most organizations have a formal process for obtaining stuff. You may be required to fill out a form and get your supervisor's approval for the requisition. Then when the request is approved, the stuff magically appears. Here are a few examples of other ways to get stuff:

- Go through the proper channels. Your supervisor knows the stuff is necessary for you to perform your duties.
- Look for substitutes. For example, what if your desk chair is not comfortable? Chairs are very expensive, and your supervisor may not be able to approve any purchases above $200. Look around in empty office spaces all over your office building. If you locate a better chair,

immediately ask your supervisor if you can make a switch—scrounge with authority!

- Locate the storage spaces for equipment such as computers, printers, lights, office furniture, etc. Identify and befriend the person who controls the storage spaces. Buying lunch is not bribery.
- Every organization has a person who is the champion scrounge. Use this person for unusual requests. Again, buying lunch is not bribery!
- Stationery cabinets (most organizations have one) typically are managed through a free access system. Remember, this is not your personal stationery supply source. It belongs to your company.

If these processes work, continue to use them. However, in some organizations this process does not work well and you might have to resort to using alternative methods. Of course, outright stealing is illegal. But scrounging—performed correctly—often is an accepted practice.

> When I was working as a factory shop foreman, my department was in desperate need of a fork truck. After all, the factory floor size exceeded 3 million square feet. My supervisor said he could not afford to purchase a new fork truck. So one night, my co-workers and I "appropriated" a fork truck from a

remote part of the factory. The truck was not in use, and was serviceable. We quickly gave it a new paint job and put it to work. This was a significant scrounge! We had asked for one using the proper channels but were refused. Later, when the supervisor toured the department and saw the fork truck, he never questioned that there suddenly was a new piece of equipment—he was more concerned with productivity.

3. YOUR WORKSPACE

Personalizing

Most organizations allow employees to personalize their workspaces. However, as an employee, you do not own your workspace: It belongs to the company and is on loan to you. The organization's professional appearance is reflected, in part, by the way you personalize your workspace. Therefore, it is important to understand your organization's guidelines regarding workspace decoration. Ask your supervisor if there are specific rules. If there are no rules, look around at the workspaces of your co-workers and follow their lead.

Consider these issues:

- Hanging pictures or posters in certain areas may be potential fire hazards.
- Do not display sexually explicit materials. This is sexual harassment—it is offensive and it is illegal.

Surviving Your Career

- It is typically acceptable to display family pictures. Bear in mind that it's probably not necessary to have one picture for every year of your children's lives.
- Maintaining live plants may be a problem. Some co-workers may have allergies to certain plants, and think about how your plants will be cared for if you are out of the office: No one wants to walk past a dying or dead plant, nor do most co-workers want to provide life support for your decorations.
- Realize that your desk is really not your desk—your employer has the right to look in your desk, file cabinets, or other storage containers. Therefore, don't store anything in your workspace you wouldn't want your supervisor to see.

A slob's workspace is similar to a junkyard. Piles of papers, magazines, food containers, possibly product samples, and tools are strewn all throughout the workspace. If there is a guest chair in the workspace, it is piled high with debris.

If the slob is running machinery, the equipment is a mess and appears poorly maintained. A slob's computer files also appear haphazard. The computer runs out of memory because files never are deleted or stored externally. The file system is disorganized and the slob is a master of using the "search" feature to find old files. Office efficiency is haphazard at best because the slob spends inordinate amounts of time locating the next work item. Of course, this description is an exaggeration, but you have to ask yourself: Do I want to have a reputation for being the office slob?

A neatnik, on the other hand, is the complete opposite of the office slob. Walking into a neatnik's workspace, you would find only the appropriate paperwork on the desk. All work is stacked into clearly labeled project or event piles. The guest chair is inviting and empty of debris. There are no accumulations of obsolete paper or electronic files. Computer files are logically organized, clearly labeled, and contain only that data that is critical to maintain. Equipment in the workspace is clean and well maintained. Here is an efficient worker who always produces a quality product or service on time.

4. CHOOSING YOUR RABBI

This is not a religious discussion. In the workplace, a rabbi is a mentor who becomes your champion. I have borrowed the term rabbi from an old police television show, "Hill Street Blues." A "rabbi" is a person who will take you under his or her wing and provide encouragement, criticism, and guidance.

Your advancement in your organization will depend on other people recognizing your achievements and recommending you for new positions. It's possible that a rabbi may select you.

However, if it becomes apparent after a few months on the job that you have not been selected, become proactive. Identify someone who seems to have power, influence, and respect in the organization. This person doesn't necessarily have to be popular, but should be recognized as an effective leader. You can begin to build a relationship by asking thoughtful and carefully considered questions, then continue to ask for advice about how you should approach a task (even if you may already have an approach of your own). The key is to show this leader you have initiative and are motivated to learn. If this person asks you to do something, jump to complete the task, even if he or she not your supervisor. Continue to develop the relationship by demonstrating your worthiness and enthusiasm. Over time, this person will naturally become your rabbi. You eventually may have more than one rabbi—more is better than none.

> *When I was a young quality engineer, out of undergraduate school only three years, my desk happened to be directly outside of the door of the Quality Manager's office, who was my own boss' supervisor. As you would expect, this manager stopped at my desk to assign little tasks. I made it a point never to question whether the task was within my job description. I simply completed the task quickly and reported*

back the results. This manager became my rabbi for the 11 years I remained at that location. In less than two years I was working directly for him as a supervisor. He was able to guide me through several rough times and was supportive when I was offered other promotions.

Chapter II BASIC SURVIVAL SKILLS

A. SURVIVING A FINANCIAL CRISIS

Most of this book was written prior to the onset of the latest recession, however the contents still apply. Surviving during any recession is difficult. If the organization employing you goes out of business you are out of work, but could still be on a career track. If the organization remains in business, your career may stall. You have to understand the need to keep your head down and do any work assignment that comes your way at any pay. Remember, recessions do not last forever.

B. NEED TO KNOW

1. ETHICS

Code of Conduct

Many organizations have a written Code of Conduct that all employees must read. A Code of Conduct can be as simple as a one-paragraph statement or as complex as multiple pages addressing a wide range of subjects. It essentially informs the employee of company policy on subjects such as stealing, lying, cheating, breaking laws, drug use, alcohol and sex. On your first day on the job, you may be asked to read and then sign the Code of Conduct, acknowledging that you have read and understood it. Organizations take the Code of Conduct very seriously, so you should assimilate the principles of the Code of

Conduct and behave accordingly from your first day on the job. Bringing a new person into an organization at any level is expensive and employers do not want to fire an employee after taking the time (and the expense) to train him or her—especially for a breach of conduct that is spelled out in the Code.

There is no middle ground when it comes to business ethics. Many ethics infractions can quickly become legal issues. For example, if you steal company property, you will be subject to a criminal charge. If you physically attack someone on the job, you will be arrested and fired. If you ask for a bribe or accept a bribe, you will eventually be caught and fired.

Many years ago several employees of General Electric and Westinghouse were found guilty of having discussions concerning the prices of their mutual products. Because discussing the price of products with competitors is against the law, the Federal Government prosecuted and penalties were pronounced against the organizations and individuals involved.

There are also potential legal penalties that often involve organizations that perform work for the Federal Government, such as companies who sell products to the Department of Defense (DOD). The DOD or Justice Department to this day continues to seek out people who either offer bribes or accept bribes that affect the cost of products sold to the DOD.

Years ago, I knew people who worked for an organization that made equipment for the military. When it was discovered that they had accepted significant gifts from suppliers, the Government penalized them by involving the IRS. These people eventually were indicted for income tax fraud and went to jail.

Business norms

The subject of ethics goes beyond a company's Code of Conduct. And, if your organization does not have a written Code of Conduct, you must assume there are generally accepted standards (norms) of behavior with which you must comply. There are business norms that are still considered ethical standards. Business norms are accepted practices for dealing fairly when conducting business with employees, customers, and suppliers. (Many unions were formed during the 19th and 20th century to influence management that did not treat their employees fairly.) Customers should be able to expect fair treatment if they have complaints or questions. There also are norms when dealing with suppliers. For example:

Suppose you were a buyer and had been working with one of your suppliers to achieve a cost reduction. In an effort to help you lower costs, the supplier performed a significant amount of design and process development work for you. After the supplier reported the results of this advance work, you sent out requests for bids. Eventually, you ended up giving the job to a new supplier who quoted a lower price but who had not performed any development work.

Sure, the new bid was lower, but you did two things wrong: First, you totally disregarded the work your first supplier did for you. After all, he believed he would continue supplying the parts once he had helped with the design work. Second, even when you had a lower bid, you did not go back to the first supplier to discuss the lower bid. In this example, you demonstrated poor business ethics and could also have been held liable for the first supplier's bill for development costs.

Sarbanes-Oxley Act

If you work for a public company, you will also learn about the Sarbanes-Oxley Act (SOA). SOA imposes a new level of ethics for reporting financial results that affect many organizational levels in public business. It's important to know if these laws affect your position and make certain you know the procedures and processes necessary to comply with them. Congress passed this law as a result of the Enron fiasco.

Starting in 1987, Enron (a large energy company) began a pattern of falsifying records in order to show unrealistically high profits. This creative reporting was aimed at raising the stock price, which certainly helped make Enron's executives very wealthy. Eventually, the facts were made public, and the Federal Government arrested and prosecuted several executives.

Public companies today may still try to get around the rules, but most companies have become very conservative in this regard. If you are responsible for falsifying a financial record that affects the organization's statement of public financial results, you will be a problem to be eliminated.

Sexual harassment

Sexual harassment is a moral, social, and legal issue that organizations must address with their employees or face both criminal and civil penalties. Your best defense is to never approach the line of harassment with either men or women. There is a long list of activities you should avoid, including:

- Touching people, even if it is your personal habit to do so.
- Telling jokes with sexual content.
- Using sex as a means of coercion with co-workers for probable advancement, compensation, or favors.

If your organization does not offer training about those specific activities, the U.S. Equal Employment Opportunity

Commission (available on the Internet) provides the necessary details. Being thoroughly informed on this issue may very well allow you to survive your career. One offense, even if you eventually are proven innocent, can destroy your career. This actually happened to a friend of mine:

> *A woman accused a friend of mine of sexual harassment. Although my friend produced witnesses that disproved the allegations, he still lost because the plaintiff was going to sue his employer if appropriate action was not taken. My friend lost his career.*

2. SICK AND PERSONAL DAYS

Most, but not all, organizations have formal policies regarding both sick and personal days. A sick day differs from a personal day. A sick day is a day off to be used when the employee is ill, such as with a bad cold or an injured back. If you wake up one morning feeling tired after partying the night before, do not plan on taking a sick day. However, with today's technology, many workers can work from home even when they do not feel well enough to go in to work. A personal day is time off allowed for necessary personal commitments, such as to see a lawyer, meet with your child's teacher, or go to a doctor's appointment.

Organizations may have either open or fixed sick and personal day programs. A fixed program has a set number of either sick or personal days for a given period (e.g., per month or per year). Most of these plans increase the number of days as your years with the company progress. In some organizations, an employee may carry over unused days from one year to the next. Open programs do not specify a quantity of sick or personal days. They leave the use of either to the discretion of employee and expect him or her to be ethical and professional.

My brother worked for the Federal Government. When he retired, he had accumulated approximately 300 unused sick days. He was compensated for the unused time using an established formula.

Your employer gives you the right to use these days within reason, and how you ultimately use them can affect survivability. My son recently asked me if the use of sick days would affect his status in his organization. My answer was "yes." If he were truly ill, his co-workers would not want him to come to work and possibly infect them, so he should stay home and get well. I also recommended that he only use sick days when absolutely necessary.

Eventually, habitual users of unwarranted sick or personal time get noticed. Some organizations have policies that demand a doctor's note after an employee has taken a given amount of sick time. That means you have to find a doctor to write a note explaining why it was necessary for you to stay home in bed. Imagine the cost of that process. Finally, if the pattern of absences continues, most supervisors will come to the conclusion that they need a full-time person instead of a part-time person—you will become a memory. The same is true for personal days. Therefore, if your company offers a set number of sick or personal days, try hard not to use these days unnecessarily.

> **Rule # 3 Use sick or personal days only when absolutely necessary**

3. RELIGION AND POLITICS

Of course, you have the right to practice your religion and vote for the candidate of your choice. Because the success of your career will depend on the cooperation of others, your workplace is not the place to argue about religion or even hint that your religion is superior to that of your co-workers. It's best just to leave these subjects outside the front door of your workplace.

Religion

It is acceptable to participate in religious observances, even if they are not listed as company holidays. Simply inform your supervisor ahead of time that you want to observe a particular holiday and that you will attend services. Your supervisor may not like it, but the Supreme Court has already ruled in your favor. Now, this might mean you could be subject to future adverse attention. The attention may be connected to your taking too many sick or personal days. If you have not abused the use of sick or personal days, you won't have a problem. It may never come to the point where you have to seek protection under the law, but if it does, you will need evidence. However, I recommend the following: Keep a dairy that documents any comments made by your supervisor concerning your practice of your religion, and also include the names of those who also may have overheard these comments.

Imposing your religious beliefs on others at the workplace is unacceptable. Your workspace belongs to the organization, so before you hang or post a religious article in your workspace, find out if there are any rules against it. Christmas decorations are no longer considered a demonstration of religious observance, but if you start to construct a large manger scene in your work area, someone may object to this kind of display. Use common sense and understand that there are many different religions represented in the workforce.

Politics

Your choice of a politician or political party is personal, but don't campaign for elected officials in the office. Remember, your working hours belong to the organization that employs you, including your break time. In addition, your political opinions probably will differ from other co-workers. The last thing an employer wants is a group of people arguing politics and not performing their paid duties. Finally, your personal opinions may differ radically from the people who control your future. Jeopardizing your future over political convictions is a mistake. Displaying campaign posters on company grounds probably is against company rules. Yes, having a casual discussion about how the country, state, county, or town is being run is probably OK at lunch time, but it is not acceptable to get into heated discussions with co-workers concerning your likes or dislikes of certain elected officials. Do it outside of the workplace so it won't interfere with day-to-day business.

On the road

If you travel for the organization to different parts of the country or the world, it is not a good idea to bring up the subject of politics or religion. If you visit a Muslim country, it could become dangerous very quickly if you start to argue about religious differences with someone who follows one of the more radical forms of the religion. Discussing politics publicly in China may result in a very unhappy situation for you with the Chinese police. Therefore, whenever you travel, be careful about expressing your opinions about religion, human rights, and politics.

4. E-MAIL, INTERNET, AND TELEPHONE

Let's assume that you use a computer with unlimited Internet access and e-mail when you're on the job. You are provided with this access so you can conduct the business of the organization. Let's also assume that you use this computer for personal e-mails to friends and relatives, Internet searches for airplane ticket prices, movies, etc. Using the computer for personal business may violate company policy and your organization probably has the ability to monitor your online activity. Most organizations today understand that when employees misuse computers, productivity is affected. At work, using the telephone and a computer is not private. When you have to gossip, do it after you go home.

E-mail

Employees can also overuse e-mail while on company time. Remember, talking face-to-face may solve a problem faster than starting a volley of e-mails back and forth. Sending out e-mails and sending copies to half the people in the organization is a waste of time. Copy only the people who have to take action. If it is simply an e-mail to report status, only copy the people who are actively interested in the project. Don't use e-mail to report poor performance or to discuss illegal activities and safety concerns. E-mails can become legal records that can be used in a legal action. Remember, you may think you can erase an e-mail, but true experts can almost always recover the message.

Internet

Avoid these absolute workplace "E-Sins" to protect your career. You shall not:

- Run an online auction business.
- Send out IP (Intellectual Property). This not only violates your organization's Code of Conduct, it also is considered theft and is a criminal offense.
- Gamble online.
- Look at pornography online.
- Spend hours surfing the Web.

- Spend hours corresponding about matters not related to business.
- Download programs from the Web to your office computer. These downloads may contain viruses, and some may interfere with company software already loaded onto your computer.
- Maintain a blog where you can post personal opinions that may affect your organization.
- Send e-mails to friends or associates where you name your organization as possibly violating laws.

Telephone

Your organization owns the telephone system and has the legal right to monitor its use. Therefore, you should limit your telephone use to business only. While most organizations realize that employees will use their telephones for some personal communications, it's important to remember that many of the "shall not's" from the "E-Sins" list also apply to telephone use.

When you leave a phone message, always be polite, speak clearly, and leave your telephone number. Speakerphones are also are very useful, but please remember you may have office neighbors who do not want to listen to your telephone conversation. Therefore, it you have to use a speakerphone setup, either close the door, or go to a conference room.

5. RAISING MONEY IN THE OFFICE

At work, it seems that someone is always selling their children's Girl Scout Cookies®, Little League® candy, or church raffle tickets, etc. Unless there are written rules in your organization's employee rules or Code of Conduct, no one will take issue. That is, unless the person selling is the supervisor or manager of the work area, then people may feel obligated to buy. If you are in a position of authority, it's best not to embarrass your people with having to make this choice. You'll be better off putting $50 into your child's envelope and calling it a day.

Raising money at work for political parties or a candidate probably is unethical, so don't even think about doing that. Here is an extraction from an organization's Code of Conduct on this subject:

Employees must not pressure, either directly or indirectly, other employees to make political contributions or to participate in support of a political party or candidate.

Raising money for a good cause, such for the victims of a natural disaster like Hurricane Katrina, usually is acceptable in the workplace. However, the organizer could simply post a sign on the bulletin board and encourage people to contribute money to a national aid organization such as the American Red Cross™. This method encourages the co-worker to make an anonymous contribution without pressure, there is no disruption of daily business, and no exchange of cash at the office involved. Use caution if you choose to be in charge of accepting and passing along the donated money to the deserving organization. You might be the most honest person in the world, but it's possible a doubting co-worker could accuse you of pocketing the donated funds.

Raising money for a co-worker in need is a noble cause, and unfortunately the funds often must be collected quickly. In this case, just make it known you are collecting money because Harry's son is in need of an operation and his medical insurance does not cover all of the costs. This is more a personal issue than asking for money for a general charity or group. Many employees can identify with those in a tight financial spot and are often willing to give what they can afford. The possibility of a suspicious co-worker accusing you of stealing the money is remote. Make certain you deliver the money quickly.

If you are a part-time representative for a company such as Avon®, good luck to you, but don't run your business at work. It's OK to sell to your co-workers, but conduct your business outside of normal working hours and deliver your products so as to not interfere with your job.

6. GAMBLING AND OFFICE POOLS

Review your organization's employee handbook or Code of Conduct. There probably is something in these documents about running gambling pools on company premises. You say, "So what? Everyone has sports pools. What else do you do for the Super Bowl or March Madness?" The truth is: You are risking criticism for violating the organization's rule on gambling. So let someone else in the organization run the pool. If you want to put your initials on a square and donate $5.00, go ahead. More than likely, you'll find your boss' initials somewhere on the square. No harm, no foul.

Gambling is a personal choice. However, if you choose to take advantage of the multitude of avenues available for gambling, don't access them from your workplace. Playing cards, shooting craps for money, or being a bookie on company premises is not a good idea. Using the office computer to play gamble in the Internet is another taboo, as is using the office telephone to place bets. First, you are risking your own money, because the house always wins in the end. Second, you are using your organization's resources improperly (See section: "E-mail, Internet, and telephone"). Sure, other people may do it, but let them risk their livelihoods and careers.

7. DRUGS, ALCOHOL, AND CIGARETTES

Drugs and your career do not mix. If you plan to use drugs either away from the office or at the workplace, the game will be over. Some organizations perform random drug tests. There probably are company protocols for dealing with a positive test, but in the end, your career will not survive.

Drinking alcoholic beverages is legal, of course, if done in moderation. However, a conviction for driving under the influence of alcohol (DUI) or negligent homicide due to drunk driving will ruin your career. The DUI may only result in you loosing your driver's license. But if your behavior causes a death, you probably will visit a new residence—jail—and life, as you know it will be over.

Smoking cigarettes is a health hazard to you and those around you. Your co-workers may not care if you smoke your way into a casket: They just do not want to be near you when you smoke. Many states have passed legislation banning smoking in public places, which includes office and factory buildings. In states where there is no legislation, some organizations have taken bold steps by implementing the ban themselves. The Supreme Court has already ruled that some organizations can force employees to not only stop smoking at work, but they may outlaw all smoking, including at home. In those organizations, if you smoke, you will be fired.

If your organization allows you to smoke in a designated area outside of a building, go ahead. But taking too many smoking breaks will be evaluated as part of your overall performance. You might not get a reprimand, but promotions, nice raises, or bonuses probably won't come your way if you take too much time out of your workday to ruin your health. Finally, some co-workers may not even want to be around you if you are a smoker. Frankly speaking, smokers stink.

8. SEX AND THE OFFICE

> **Rule # 4 Do not have sex on company property, and avoid having sex with a co-worker, anywhere.**

You might think it sounds like fun to have an affair, but the risks are huge. You should simply avoid it at all costs. Starting and ending a relationship with a co-worker may introduce stress into the work place and could certainly affect your performance. Here are a few critical issues to think about:

- Be certain you cannot be accused of sexual harassment or are not putting the other person at risk of being

accused of sexual harassment. If either of those scenarios occurs, your association with the organization will end eventually, depending on who accuses whom of what.
- In spite of the possibility of sexual harassment, you both have to work for the same organization. If one of you is married and conflict ensues, you will carry that stress into the workplace, which may create a serious problem. Just imagine your spouse arriving at your workplace and loudly accusing you of having an affair. To say the least, it could be embarrassing and disruptive. The same might also be true if both of you are single and the relationship fails. You cannot bring these problems to work with you.

B. GETTING ALONG
1. COOPERATION IS THE KEY

> **Rule # 5 Be polite.**

- Your success will not depend on your abilities alone. You will be successful only if you can cooperate with your co-workers, suppliers, customers, government officials, and others to get the job done. Some examples:
- When making a request, say "please." Follow up with "thank you" when someone does something for you.

- Go out of your way to let others know when someone else does something that benefits you. This will win you future cooperation points with others.
- When you have been assigned to develop a new process or revise an existing process, remember that processes depend on people. Take the time to discuss the prospective process with the people who are involved. Work to gain consensus. You might even find that others have better ideas than you have. If this is the case, then give them the credit and thank them. You will only get away with dictating a process if your organizational layer allows you sufficient authority to issue an edict without consulting the doers. However, there will be times when a manager or supervisor has to demand a process change simply because there is a business need. This is where the saying, "the buck stops here" applies.
- When co-workers ask for your help, try not to turn them away without offering some assistance. The tables could turn and you could need their help someday. Take the time to listen to the request and then mutually work out how you can help (even if you are busy with your own work). Never say, "That's not my job." Remember that old saying: Never piss off a person on the way up, because you may meet the same person on the way down.

- Someday, a customer needing assistance may contact you. He or she may have reached you by mistake, maybe you have absolutely nothing to do with the request. Whatever the circumstances, do not turn the customer away. Listen to the request, inform the customer you do not have the ability to provide assistance, but you will immediately search for the correct person to help them. Obtain a call back number and then immediately take the time to search for the correct person. Give the contact number to this co-worker, but follow-up with a telephone call back to the customer informing them they will be contacted. Finally, ask the customer to get back to you if the proper contact is not made. This customer will never forget your cooperation and probably will go the extra mile and tell others of your efforts.

- > **Rule # 6 Never turn your boss away—for any reason.**

Cooperating with your boss is important. The boss will give you orders, make requests of your time, ask for help, or simply want to use you as a sounding board. Some of these demands of your time may be little tests to see how you conduct yourself outside of your comfort zone.

2. OFFICE POLITICS

Office politics are a reality. It's important to understand that when people play this game, their purpose is to position themselves to take advantage of opportunities that will lead to additional compensation or power. It's acceptable to be either an ***observer*** or a ***player*** when it comes to office politics. Each has its risks and rewards. Then it's up to you to simply decide which you chose to be and to determine how the game is played in your organization.

Observers

People who are observers keep their opinions to themselves and simply do their jobs. They usually are considerate of their co-workers and they do not attempt to always play up their accomplishments to superiors. During organization social functions, an observer does not make a special attempt to stand or sit next to the president. The observer gets the job done, but is willing to watch the world go by. Observers will assume a neutral position and typically will advance in their career based upon their own achievements. In other words they will not be either hurt or helped as a result of office politics.

Players

People who are players take every opportunity to be "seen"— whether or not they actually are doing a good job. Players always offer opinions in meetings—whether or not the comments are relevant. They volunteer for special projects— even if they never intend to actually do any work. They make a special effort to drop names and be close to people with power. They often send blind copies of e-mails to upper management when communicating important issues. Players can be dangerous simply because, when someone in management receives their input, they may consider the input as factual data. And in many cases the data from a player is biased only towards himself. The cartoon series Dilbert® often portrays management as sponges, soaking up any information coming to them. The problem is how they interpret the information and the subsequent actions they take. So the player can be dangerous to observers and other players. Therefore, beware of how you interact with players.

What happens to a player? In some organizations, their efforts pay off and they are rewarded with more power or money. This is unfortunate because these successes often come at the expense of more deserving people. In other organizations, upper management is more enlightened, and understands the office politics game, so the player is managed appropriately.

3. BUREAUCRATIC NONSENSE

So what is bureaucratic nonsense (BN)?

Your organization has decided too much time is wasted in meetings throughout the corporation. Someone at headquarters has hired a consulting company, at some enormous cost, to develop a training program for all salaried people in the corporation. The purpose of the training course is to teach people to conduct more efficient meetings. The length of the training course is two full days. This is total BN.

The larger the organization, the more bureaucratic nonsense is required of employees. There simply are more opportunities for larger organizations to spawn people who dream up and get away with launching these types of initiatives. If you are in a small organization and your supervisor came from a large organization, there will be some of the same nonsense. This will happen because the manager doesn't know any better since he was able to launch "BN" in his old organization. Smaller organizations cannot survive with too much "BN" simply because of the size of the business.

Here are some more examples of bureaucratic nonsense:

- All reports have to use a specific font.
- Everyone in the organization has to capture one good idea per week and pass it up to the boss.
- As a result of the probability of a pandemic flu outbreak in the United States, a plan must be developed describing business continuity within the next week.
- Once a year, all employees have to confirm they have read all of the company policies.
- You must use the organization's specified method for booking travel, even if you know you can save money using an alternative method.
- All desks must be free of any paper at the end of the workday.

This list can go on and on. The cartoon strip Dilbert® is the world's best archive for lessons in bureaucratic nonsense.

What can be done about this nonsense? Fighting bureaucratic nonsense may harm your career because someone at a higher pay grade probably imposed the requirement. Most for-profit organizations come to understand the negative value of bureaucratic nonsense rather quickly so do not lose heart. Once the "BN" is minimized, the employees have more time and opportunity to just do their jobs.

If you work for a not-for-profit or government organization, you could have a more difficult fight. The classic not-for-profit generator of "BN" is government. We continue to read about work process methodology within the ranks of our government offices and how hard it is to achieve any improvements. Since there is no profit motivation, there is little effort given to eliminate BN. In fact it often grows. Bureaucracy seems to breed waste that creates or guarantees jobs.

4. DEALING WITH STUPID PEOPLE

The problem

The easiest way to have a bad day is to be in contact with someone who just "doesn't get it." What if you asked someone to do something simple according to an established process and he or she simply went in a different direction and came up with a strange result? Talk about frustration! Your first reaction to this situation might to jump up and down on the head of this person, yelling and screaming—"You stupid fool!" Of course, if you actually did this, you would have violated the Code of Conduct and you'd be fired.

Responding

The best way to respond is to take a step back and review the situation:

- Did you ask the right person to do the task? It is possible that the person you asked was not qualified to meet your expectations.
- What did you actually ask this person to do? Was your request hard to understand? Was it an unreasonable request?
- Is it possible that poor communication on your part was the cause of the problem in the first place?
- How did the outcome differ from your expectations?

However, if your request was made properly, you asked the right person, and your expectations still were not met, then you should calmly meet with the offender and discuss what went wrong. Talking through a situation often will solve the problem. Most reasonable people want to do a good job but frequently do not know how to get things done properly. Now, if this approach does not work, work your way up the organizational ladder, trying to communicate an understanding of the problem, but remember to have a solution. Since this involves a personnel issue, don't attack the person—address the process that makes it difficult for people to comply.

If the solution solves the problem, people in authority will be in a position to assist with implementation. The key is for you to have the facts surrounding the given situation. What was the initial issue? How was it originally handled? And what was the result? Do not embellish or attempt to malign the offender because you will be criticized for attacking the person, not the process. Your only goal is to get the job done. Let someone else in the organization conduct the public execution of the offender.

5. TRUSTING CO-WORKERS

> **Rule # 7 Don't trust your co-workers with your career.**

> **Rule # 8 The people in the Human Resources department are not your friends. They are charged with protecting the organization.**

Your career is yours to protect and, in reality, you are in competition with your co-workers for your position and advancement. This is particularly true in larger organizations. The Human Resources Department is responsible for staffing and associated activities. It is not responsible for demands for the health and happiness of individuals, but rather the welfare of the entire organization. In addition, it is charged with protecting the company from legal issues that might arise from employees. Therefore do not disclose the following things to either your co-workers or the Human Resources personnel:

- Any thoughts you may have about looking outside for alternative employment. Keep these plans to yourself until you are certain you will join a new organization.
- Your dissatisfaction with your supervisor.
- Any discussion concerning any violation of the organization's Code of Conduct. Unless you can present ironclad facts concerning another person's violation, don't raise the issue. Remember you have to continue to promote cooperation with your co-workers.
- Discussions about your current workload, either too much or not enough. If it is too much, develop plans for managing the workload. When you are successful, your supervisor will acknowledge the achievement. If you truly believe you are working too hard, leave the organization and get an easier job.
- Rumors that discuss other people or the future of the organization. Avoid being accused of starting these rumors.

- Your plans for retirement, until you are absolutely ready to take the leap.
- Complaints that you are underpaid. If you believe you are being discriminated against and have proof, first have the discussion with your supervisor and then, if necessary, Human Resources. Make sure you have the facts to support your allegations.

6. LOSING YOUR TEMPER

Those were the good old days: production meetings with people yelling, cursing, and almost fighting over production issues—a situation I call "Extreme Theory X." If you were on the receiving end of this type of disagreement, you might not miss those days at all. Those were the days when you lived in fear of a tyrannical supervisor whose habit was to yell and scream commands to any and all employees to get the results needed. The sad fact of those times was that many businesses encouraged supervisors to be Extreme Theory X managers. Fortunately, the days of conducting business with a yelling and screaming match are over. When you disagree with someone in today's business climate, losing your temper is unacceptable. Today, the usual course is to have a rational discussion based on the facts. If you go further and get into a physical altercation, it's my guess you will be fired or suspended. If you are the aggressor and you injure another person in a fight, expect to have a civil suit filed against you. Using foul language also is not tolerated in most business environments, and men who use foul language in the presence of women (or vise versa!) may end up on the wrong side of a sexual harassment suit.

If you find yourself in a situation where you might lose your temper, it is best to stop, calmly listen to what the other person is saying, and write down the facts as they are presented to you. If you disagree but are not in a position to argue your point, it is best to keep quiet. If you have a defendable position to refute the comments, do so after that person is finished stating his or her position. Calmly say that you disagree and then give your reasons. One of the easiest business practices is to "agree to disagree." After the confrontation, collect your evidence, and if you believe you need a public forum, call a meeting to present your case with all parties affected by the situation. Let your supervisor be the tiebreaker.

7. OVERACHIEVING

My brother and I learned our work ethic from our father, who instructed us to finish a task quickly, once it was assigned. My brother was a union plumber who worked on major construction projects. Years ago, he was working on a project expanding the U.S. Military Academy at West Point, NY. He was given an assignment to install plumbing fixtures in a dormitory restroom. He began to work, proceeding with the job as he would with any task. After several hours, a few other plumbers approached him and told him to slow down. They implied that he was working much too fast and if he wanted to stay healthy, he should listen. My brother immediately slowed down and worked the same pace as his co-workers. He remained on that job for several years.

The definition of overachieving might not be as I described above about my brother, nor may it be physically harmful to your health. Overachieving is in the eyes of the beholder and how the impact of overachieving reflects on others. You might think that being an overachiever would benefit your career. Whether or not overachieving will be valuable really depends on the culture of your organization and the number of overachievers who work there. Here's why:

- If you are an overachiever in a small organization where there are few duplicate positions or skill sets, you are more likely to be accepted by your co-workers because you probably will not be competing with them for advancement. Your co-workers probably won't feel threatened and your supervisor may perceive your efforts as an indication of excellent performance. If you want to be recognized as having the potential for promotion, then you should try to be an overachiever. Just measure out the amount of your achievement based upon the impact it has on others in the organization, then act accordingly. Also remember the story about my brother, and make certain your co-workers are not unreasonable.

- In a large organization where there are many duplicate positions and skill sets, you have to be more careful with showmanship—putting yourself in the position of always being the first person in a meeting to present the "next" best idea, or making certain everyone knows you have finished an assignment, and you that have solved world hunger. Large organizations tend to be very competitive places. There frequently are limited opportunities for promotion, and raises tend to be averaged over large numbers of people. Therefore, it's not a good idea to step over the bodies of your co-workers (or practicing showmanship) to make an impression. There is always a risk of a supervisor simply raising the performance measurement bar for all people doing the same job.

One of my first industrial jobs was to perform a stopwatch time study in a meatpacking factory. I observed people performing their work and timed their movements as they processed the product. Then I performed calculations based on what I had observed and created a time standard of the amount of product they produced. If anyone had wanted to "showboat," or work very fast, it would have affected the result of the study and then everyone would have had to work at that speed from that time forward.

Certainly you should strive for excellence for personal gain, but temper your achievement based upon the effect it will have on your co-workers. Will being an overachiever always result in more compensation or a promotion?

Studies by the Hay Group (a respected global human resources management consulting firm headquartered in Philadelphia) show that, since 2000, raises in the United States have been meager. Most large organizations have limited raises to around 3–3.5 percent annually, even though inflation has been stable and the supply of workers to fill positions in many disciplines exceeds the demand. Therefore, organizations tend to spread the increases rather evenly across their employees.

If a supervisor has 10 people directly reporting to him or her, the likelihood of the overachiever getting a fantastic raise is low because that raise would lower the raises for the other 9 people. The overachiever may get a 4–5 percent raise, but would probably never get a 10 percent raise.

The other factors to consider are pay scales and pay ranges. The supervisor will always be concerned where the employee is within the pay level range. Most organizations that maintain formal pay levels with assigned ranges exercise strict controls for where compensation falls within a given pay level's range.

For example, consider the engineer whose position is considered a Level 14. Then assume that the lowest compensation level for that level is $60,000 and the high end is $73,200. If the employee is currently paid $72,900 and the supervisor wants to give the employee a 3.5 percent raise, the Human Resources Department will probably deny that raise. Therefore, when the employee gets too close to the higher limit, his or her pay may be frozen, even though he or she is an overachiever. The supervisor may be frustrated because the employee may simply seek a new job.

Promotions generally come as a result of many factors, but does the probability of getting a promotion increase if you are consistently an overachiever? Yes, if you can sustain the high level of achievement over time. There also are other factors used to consider a person for a promotion besides output, as discussed in other sections of this book.

8. BORED—LOOKING BUSY

There may come a time when you simply run out of work to do. You may have many projects underway and you are waiting for something to happen, so you simply do not have any work in front of you. You have two choices:

- If you think the problem is long-term, ask for more work. However, you should only ask for more work if you know for certain that more work exists. If you ask for more work when there isn't any, your supervisor may simply think: "I don't need this person any longer. Good-bye." The alternative is to have an honest discussion with your supervisor if you have determined there is another open position in the organization that fits your skills and career goals. This indeed is a gamble on your part, because you have to be confident the organization considers you valuable enough to retain you.
- If you know the problem is short-term, sit tight and wait for your own work to become more active. If you are in this mode, the most important thing to watch is your attitude, because boredom causes stress and anxiety. If this happens, you should behave as though everything is "business as usual." Don't complain at this point because it only a short-term problem. You do not want to be labeled as a whiner. If you choose to wait it out, try the following:
- Never admit to anyone you have no work. Just look busy.
- Clean up your files, both hardcopy and computer files.

- Clean up your entire workplace.
- Look for any online training your company may offer and start on that. This will at least show initiative on your part to keep developing your skills and acquiring knowledge.
- Even though considered a "no-no", if your computer screen is not visible to others, correspond with friends. At least it will look like you are working. Think about writing a book or and article on a favorite subject. Then do it, because it will look like you are busy. Just be careful of using of the computer for looking busy, since someone may be monitoring its use.
- Do not sit back and snooze, make long and loud telephone calls to friends, wander the hallways; drop into other people's workspaces, balance your checkbook, or do other personal financial busy work.

CHAPTER III GETTING THE JOB DONE

A. DAY IN THE LIFE

1. COMPLETING TASKS

When you get an assignment, determine the performance expectations:

- Write down the task you were given.
- Ask for an explanation of what you are expected to deliver from the task. A deliverable may be a report, a completed project (which by itself has a deliverable), a purchased item delivered to an assigned location, or simply moving the mountain of rocks from one location to another.
- Determine the expected completion date or deadline. You should always complete the task prior to the required date. If this means you will need to work hard long hours, Saturdays, and Sundays, so be it. This is why you are the worker and not the leader at this point. Because this task probably will be one of the many projects you already are working on at the same time, plan to prioritize your time.
- Start to develop a plan for completing the task and meeting the expectations.

The plan consists of:

- All the steps it will take to complete the task.
- Dates for completion of each step.
- Sources of assistance or support.
- Necessary tools or equipment.
- Training required to finish the task properly.
- Known safety issues.
- A list of unknowns (e.g., questions for additional information and where you might obtain the answers).
- A list of assumptions. The assumptions have to be turned into facts. It is best to document all of those facts that form a foundation for completing the task.

Review your project plan with your customer and/or supervisor. Using a planned approach that includes a documented project plan will demonstrate to your supervisor that you approach tasks in an organized manner, that you respect deadlines, and you plan to deliver the completed task on time.

Finally, all of the documentation and planning is worthless unless you deliver the end result to a customer who is satisfied with the product. Don't be afraid to have a customer satisfaction discussion with the customer. This is a learning opportunity upon which you can build future tasks—in other words, did you do a good job? This review also will demonstrate your professionalism to that specific customer. If you have completely satisfied this person, he or she is more apt to call on you again for new work, and also will provide a good reference if and when you are ever seeking another position.

2. MEETINGS

When you are invited to a meeting, take the time to understand the purpose and determine if you will have a role in the meeting. Generally, there is a business purpose to a business meeting. (Occasionally, you may run across some meetings that are called by people who have political motivations or who simply want to demonstrate their personal importance.) If you received an agenda with the meeting notice, take it with you to the meeting. Be on time and take a seat at the table. Do not take a backbench seat.

> *A backbench is a term from Great Britain's House of Commons. The chamber used for the House of Commons is not large, and Ministers with low seniority are given a seat in the back.*

Your situation is different because you want to be seen and heard. Therefore, do not take a seat where you are not noticed. Introduce yourself to people you do not know. Now is not the time to be shy. Find out if minutes of the meeting will be taken. If necessary, keep your own minutes. You might be asked for your opinion, so do your homework. If you are prepared with data and understand the subject matter, feel free to contribute, but allow the host to lead the meeting. If you had been assigned to report on an action item, be prepared to do so.

Watch the interaction between participants. Remember office politics is a reality. Notice how people respond during the conversations: Who goes on the attack? Who is defensive? Who is not prepared? Who shows up late? Who is rude? Who is eloquent? Who is respectful? Whom do others recognize for accomplishments? These observations will help with personal interactions in the future.

The following tips will help you remain attentive during meetings:

- Avoid seat fatigue and a case of "fidgets." (Obviously everyone's body is different and how you adapt to a given chair for a given period of time is different with each meeting room.) The best way to avoid fidgeting is to stay focused on the meeting, take notes, work at listening and, if appropriate, engage in the conversation. But don't have side conversations that might disturb the meeting.
- If you need a restroom break during the meeting, it's OK to just get up and leave.

- Avoid eating during the meeting unless you know it is listed as a meeting with a meal. Sipping drinks such as coffee or water is acceptable. If you bring a snack, it's polite to provide enough for everyone attending.
- My recommendation is to stand up during long meetings if you can do so without disturbing the meeting, or at the very least, stretch you legs under the table.

When you call for a meeting, determine beforehand what you expect to accomplish. Produce an agenda and invite only those people who are relevant to the topic and tasks at hand. Do not invite the supervisors of the invitees in order to impress the supervisors. Having more people than necessary at a meeting may hamper your efforts to meet your objectives. Avoid planning a meeting that will take longer than an hour. Start your meeting on time, conduct discussions, take notes, and at the end of the meeting summarize any action items. After the meeting, publish minutes and action items quickly. Your organization may have its own established format for documenting meeting minutes. If there is one, use it. If there is not, there are essential elements to a set of minutes:

- What was the subject and purpose of the meeting?
- When was it conducted?
- Who attended?

- A concise description of the discussions
- Action items, including a description of the action, person responsible for the action item and the expected completion date.

3. **WRITTEN COMMUNICATION**

Hand written notes, memos, or letters are not nearly as common or useful as they once were. In all likelihood, your organization has computers with word processing software available for this purpose. Today most written correspondence is through e-mail. E-mail seems to have even taken the place of person-to-person verbal contacts, which may be both a curse and a blessing. With e-mail, you also can attach other documents such as a project report, trip report, or analysis of data to support your communication. Always remember that content, format, spelling, and grammar all "count"—people reading your communication probably will judge you by your ability to produce a sensible, clean, accurate document.

When presenting written communication:

- Be prepared to substantiate any claims you put forth. Be sure you can defend your position using credible resource material if necessary. If you are presenting your opinion, be sure to identify it as your opinion only.

- Use your organization's prescribed formats and styles for written communication, which may include using specific fonts, colors, or layout parameters.
- Use spell check. It's a useful tool for those of us who have lost our ability to spell.
- After you have written a document, try to set it aside, for even a few minutes. Then re-read it for clarity. On occasion, it may be helpful to have someone else read it for clarity, grammar, and format.
- If your communication contains data, make certain the display of data is meaningful. Does the display provide an answer to a question? The most effective way to display data is to use a graph. Learn how to set up a graph with the correct format, data labels, coordinate scales, and titles.
- If the purpose of your communication is to document assignments to action items, always include a description of the action item, who is to carry it out, and the agreed upon completion date.
- Only send copies of e-mails to those who really need to respond to your communication.

One of the major curses of electronic communications is the ease with which you can send copies of e-mails. If you overuse this feature, you may be sending copies of your e-mail to people who are not involved in your project or issue—they probably will delete your e-mail without reading it, or if they read it, will be wasting their time. Only those few people who really need to receive the communication will take action.

Business people often do not have the time to read a lengthy document. Keep it short and to the point. If the discussion must be lengthy, include an executive summary at the beginning of the document.

When you need to send a document outside of your organization, be aware that there may be rules for reviewing the content of the document before it leaves the organization. This includes both e-mail and/or actual hard copy letters.

4. MONTHLY REPORT

A monthly report typically is the written communication tool for reporting your activities of the month. Your boss may have to provide a similar report to his or her supervisor and so on, until the organizational food chain stops at the top. These reports typically contain short descriptions of the status of projects, significant achievements, critical problems affecting performance, and general subjects affecting how the organization conducts its business. Your boss will collect other reports from his or her staff and will create another filtered report. This process will continue until the filtered, bland, and far-fetched facts reach the top manager. Your boss can select items from your report and claim credit for any success. Don't get upset—this is just how things work. The value of the department's report may or may not exist. It depends how the next person in the organization's food chain uses the information to further his or her position in the overall organization. As an example:

> *A manager collected all of the input from her direct reports, and developed a very comprehensive report of the department's activities and progress for several projects. The receiving director did not have a high regard for this particular manager, and often discounted much of what he received. The director tended to send very terse monthly reports to his immediate supervisor. Therefore, all of the time put into collecting input, selecting highlights from individual activity reports, editing, and enhancing by the manager essentially was wasted, non-value added time.*

On the other hand, the report is valuable to you because it becomes a good history of your accomplishments that you then can use for your annual performance evaluation, assuming that process has value. Save the data from the monthly reports throughout the year. Your report also becomes a valuable documentation of your accomplishments that you can use to update your resume.

Before you create your first monthly report, find out about:

- Format. Is there a specific format required for this report? Before starting your report, ask your boss to show you an activity report from a co-worker.
- Quality. Treat this report like the most important term paper in the world. It's essential to use correct English, spelling, grammar, and punctuation. Do not use this report to communicate bad news unless you also report a solution to the problem.
- Length. Your report should be just long enough to describe what you have done in the previous month.
- Do not use this report to incriminate a co-worker.
- This report should describe what you have accomplished, not what you intend to do.
- Write the report and let it sit for one night. Then proofread it the next day, before you submit it to your supervisor. After you submit the first report, ask you supervisor for a critique.

> **Rule # 9 Never turn in a report late.**

5. GIVING PRESENTATIONS

Public speaking is a requirement for many business careers. But if you are nervous about speaking in front of others, you're not alone. One of the first training requests you should make is to attend a Dale Carnegie® course where you can learn how to overcome your fear of standing up to give a presentation to any size audience.

The following critical factors will help you give successful presentations:

- Determine the purpose of the presentation.
- Determine how much time you have to give your presentation, where it will be given, and who is the intended audience?
- Prepare a presentation that will fulfill that purpose, answer relevant questions, and address pertinent issues.
- Do your research to develop content for your presentation. Most presentations typically include both verbal and visual components. The visual segment can include actual samples, slides, audio, video or some combination of those elements. Make certain the location of the presentation will have the necessary equipment and support for your program.

- When you have prepared a draft of the presentation, review the content with someone who can help you verify that you have achieved your goals and that the material is interesting and flows logically.

> **Rule # 10 Do not bore your audience.**

Regardless of your audience, a presentation will be judged as a part of your overall job performance. You are going public, even if the presentation covers a minor point. Your peers and superiors in the organization will judge your ability to develop a presentation that is based upon facts; that you are prepared to answer questions; and that you are comfortable performing in front of an audience.

Presentations also are forums for questions from the audience. You will be expected to be the expert on the presentation topic. When someone asks a question, speak directly to that person. If you are in a large room and you think others may not have heard the question, repeat the question before answering it. If you do not know the answer to the question, say so. Tell the questioner you will find the answer and will get back to him or her later with the information. Always follow up: even if it takes a telephone call or an e-mail. If action items are raised as a result of the presentation, write them down and publish them with the minutes.

Giving a presentation is not the place to win an award for style or length. Keep it short and factual. If you have a handout to distribute, make certain you have made copies for everyone. Don't forget to recognize individuals or groups who have assisted in accomplishing a task.

Always:

- Make eye contact with the audience.
- Have a back up plan in the event of equipment failure.
- Speak loudly enough for all to hear you clearly.
- Be expressive. Avoid a monotone voice.
- Dress appropriately.
- Stick to the scheduled time period for the presentation.
- Make comments and jokes in good taste.

Finally, you may get requests for copies of your electronic presentation, so have digital copies available for distribution (unless there is a copyright issue). The easiest method for distributing copies is via e-mail, as long as the file size is not too large. If the file is too large, then you may want to have CD copies available for distribution. If you do not know all of the people in your audience, simply ask those who are interested in receiving a copy to provide a business card with an e-mail address.

Always retain your own copy of the presentation because you may want to use parts of it in future presentations.

6. MAKING MISTAKES

We all make mistakes! Depending on the cultural environment of your organization, mistakes will drive learning and improvement. We're only human, and the old adage—mistakes are evidence of people doing something—definitely applies. A mistake is not a capital offense, but how the correction is managed so that you avoid new mistakes is critical. Repeatedly making mistakes—or not learning from your mistakes—could jeopardize your career.

So what should you do if you have made a mistake?

- Face the fact you made the mistake. If you ignore the problem, it will come back to haunt you.
- Quickly determine the consequences of your mistake. Will it create a safety concern? Could someone get physically hurt? Will equipment fail? Will it create a negative environmental impact? Will it create another problem or issue that could cause the legal problems for you or for the organization?
- Before you present the event or problem to anyone— if the consequences are not serious—determine how you can correct the error and minimize its effect.

- Develop a plan to avoid repeating the error in the future. Then present both the mistake and the probable solution to your supervisor.
- Treat all mistakes as a personal learning opportunity.
- Keep a personal record of your mistakes. Someday, you may be able to show how you saved the day by turning a mistake into an opportunity, even though you caused the problem. Finally, you should revisit these records from time to time as a reminder never to make the same mistake twice.

7. SAFETY

Personal safety on the job

Job safety is a serious subject. Every organization wants to avoid all accidents, especially those that result in permanent serious injury—or worse. Accidents and injuries result in loss of productivity and increased costs, and lost time injuries result in higher Workers Compensation premiums.

Many organizations have documented safety rules and formal safety programs, while other organizations simply expect their employees to use sound judgment and not get hurt on the job. In some organizations, employees who fail to comply with safety regulations may be terminated. And in some states, an injured employee can sue the employer if negligence on the part of the organization has caused the injury.

Whether your job is in a school, hospital, factory, store, or an office, take the time to identify the safety issues. Look around:

- Are exits clearly marked and accessible?
- Are fire extinguishers available?
- Are there any sharp edges that might cause you to cut yourself?
- Always use the recommended personal protective safety equipment provided for your job.
- If your organization has a safety manual, correlate the safety issues of your job with the safety manual and plan how you will stay safe.
- Take advantage of offered safety training programs.
- Take the time to learn the best escape routes for fire drills.
- If you still have concerns about safety issues, discuss them first with your co-workers and then with your supervisor. In any case, you should feel free to stop and report any unsafe activity on the job. If your organization's management does not fix an unsafe situation, you will have to decide if you will continue working in that environment or seek assistance outside of your organization.

There are avenues for assistance through government agencies such as Occupational Safety and Health Administration (OSHA). You might rectify a safety problem by doing the right thing and reporting the situation to OSHA, but you probably will endanger your career. Most employers really prefer to resolve safety issues internally. Once an issue is reported to an outside agency, the potential for the company to be exposed to increased costs and adverse publicity increases significantly. Therefore, it is far better to try to find a solution with your current employer to improve safety in your workplace.

Product safety

If you are involved with delivering products or services, take product safety very seriously. If you are not certain of your position concerning product safety, ask questions so you will understand your responsibilities. Product safety, despite its importance, is complicated and often expensive to manage.

A hospital's products are the medical services it provides, and there are numerous product safety issues associated with delivering medical services. In an organization that makes industrial equipment such as turbines, there also are issues with product safety, starting with the design of the turbine parts and how they are made.

Product liability suits are expensive to defend and often result in rather large settlements. In certain lawsuit situations, the plaintiff may go after both the employee and the organization in hopes of winning a large a reward. Fortunately, organizations realize it's less expensive in the long run to prevent product safety issues than to mitigate the consequences of a failed product that injures a customer or has other consequences, such as damaging the environment.

B. YOU AND YOUR ORGANIZATION

1. WHO ARE THE CUSTOMERS

Because every organization has a product—hardware, software, or a service—there always will be customers who want or need that product. And by buying your product, your customers actually are paying the bills that allow your organization to stay in business. Therefore, it's crucial for everyone to know who the customers are. Government employees understand that citizens are the customers who pay the bills. In the case of not-for-profit organizations, the customers are the people who benefit from the services/products of the organization.

<u>**External customers**</u>

Your external customer is any customer who directly or indirectly purchases your products or services. Your purpose and responsibility is to satisfy those customers and to have them return again and again. As soon as you join an organization, take the time to identify and understand the external customer by asking: "Who are they, and why do they use our products?" Although your position may be many process steps away from either meeting or talking to an actual customer, take the initiative to know who they are. Someday you may be able to impress someone in your organization based on this understanding.

Let's assume you work as a buyer of paper products for a company that produces greeting cards and sells them to distributors, who in turn sell to retail stores, who then finally sell to consumers. You have absolutely no contact with the external customers, but your position may affect the quality of the paper used to make the actual greeting card.

At some point in your career, you may have the opportunity meet and talk to your external customers. Remember to always be professional, courteous, and understand that many customers need the assistance of your organization in order to make purchases. And as you provide this assistance, you will benefit the company—and ultimately—your career.

Suppose you are a salesperson in a TV store. You've noticed that most customers who come in to the store have a list of questions about various models, prices, or available technologies. When you have the ability to answer their questions, respond to their needs, and listen for feedback, you can create the opportunity to guide the customer to the store's most profitable TV.

Internal customers

Your internal customer is the person or department within your organization who uses the output from your desk or workspace.

For example, if you are a receiving clerk, someone will take the packing list and compare it to an invoice from a supplier in order to pay the invoice. In this case, the user of the packing slip is your customer. The same holds true of the person waiting for the goods listed on the packing slip. That person is dependent on you to route the goods to the proper location within the facility.

Take the initiative to talk to your internal customers. Find out if they are satisfied with your product. Ask how you might improve your service in order to make their jobs easier. This simple relationship-building step will help set the stage for cooperation and collaboration in the future.

2. QUALITY AND YOU

Quality means survival for any organization. If your customers cannot use your product or are dissatisfied with the quality of the product and service you provide, they will go elsewhere. And obviously, having fewer customers means reduced business, which ultimately means needing fewer employees. However, if you are not working in your organization's Quality Assurance or Quality Control department, do you have any responsibility for quality? Yes!

> **Rule # 11 You are responsible for quality and to satisfy the requirements and expectations of your external and internal customers.**

How do you learn about quality? It is important to understand what is expected of you when it comes to quality.

- If your organization has a formal quality program or quality department, ask if there is a quality manual with procedures. Get a copy and read it so you'll understand how your position fits into the quality system as a whole.
- If there is no formal quality program, be proactive and ask your supervisor to describe the organization's quality ethic or standard.

- In either case, find out if your department has a history of causing either internal defects or customer complaints. Determine if the data shows positive or negative trends. Again, this is another way you can demonstrate initiative. If the trend is negative, find out if anyone has been assigned to investigate the root causes of the defects or complaints and to develop corrective actions.

Now, do you want to be a hero? If you are comfortable with analyzing data and determining root causes of problems, volunteer to lead an initiative to make improvements. If you have never done this type of work, ask your supervisor if he or she has ever considered launching an improvement project. It's my guess you will be invited to be on the team. This will be a great learning opportunity for you.

> **Rule # 12 Never hesitate to report a substandard product.**

The last thing any organization or employee wants is for substandard products to reach a customer. If you need to report a substandard product, do it such a way as to avoid threatening your co-workers.

The auto and toy industries often launch recalls for products. These recalls cost millions for the manufacturers and the distributors, and also result in customer dissatisfaction. But, if the products were not recalled and a personal injury or death occurred, the manufacturer would be subject to potential civil penalties. Each organization faces specific consequences if substandard products reach the customer's hands.

During the latter part of 2006, we saw a series of food recalls in the United States because of reported illnesses. Food companies began testing their products and now perform voluntary recalls. The next steps will be testing prior to distributing the products to eliminate the need for a recall.

Make certain your personal involvement is in accordance with the technical and process requirements established by your organization. If you are actually producing products, make certain you understand the product acceptance criteria. You are human and you may make a mistake and produce non-complying product. The key to your survival is to minimize mistakes.

Suppose you had a job in a factory producing electric irons that were used by consumers to iron clothing at home. Your job was to put two sub-assemblies together and then connect three sets of wires. There was acceptance criteria—

a very detailed written description of the exact steps to make the connection. The engineering department also had created a method sheet and a set of photos showing the wire connection process.

The previous operator who trained you gave you only verbal description of the methods because the written method sheets had been lost. So for your first four months on the job, you produced the assembly and wire connections according to the instructions you understood from the previous assembler. You never bothered to ask for the authorized version of the assembly method, which contained the accepted method of wire connection. Your connection method then was faulty and there wasn't a planned inspection or test process to validate your work. If your assembled irons were sold and then caused fires, property damage and personal injury could have been the unhappy result.

As a result of an investigation, your company could have been sued and required to pay a settlement in the millions of dollars. You and several others also could be named in the suit, and the company could refuse to cover your portion of the judgment because you failed to follow procedures.

3. EMBRACE THE NEXT BIG INITIATIVE

> **Rule # 13 Embrace new programs with enthusiasm.**

Most managers and executives read business books, trade magazines, and also attend conferences. Historically, these activities have launched initiatives that were destined to transform organizations. Some organizations have spent millions chasing the principles of the big initiative. Okay, what is a big initiative?

Business organizations are born, grow up and pass through many phases of life, just as people do. As a business goes through a phase, one of the executives may learn from a trade magazine of a new business principle that is "transforming" business and that has saved a specific business "piles of money." "WOW," says the first manager, "that can work in my business." This next "big initiative" then begins to take shape in another location. The manager makes a call to one of his subordinates and instructs that person to develop a plan for deploying the "big initiative" throughout the organization. So it begins, finally landing on your desk. An example of one of these situations is:

In 1979, Phillip Crosby published <u>Quality Is Free</u>. Mr. Crosby had been the Vice President and Director of Quality, at International Telephone & Telegraph. The book presented a different approach to the Quality Assurance concept for businesses at that time. However, too many executives failed to understand the true meaning of what Crosby was selling, which was the concept that quality is free once you have invested in a well-designed quality program. Many organizations launched quality programs that were not properly designed and much to their chagrin they discovered that quality is only free if you pay attention to the concepts and adequately implement a quality program.

Whether the program is properly designed and implemented is not important for this discussion. What is important is your role in any of these "big initiatives." Often these programs require extensive training. When offered, don't avoid the training, don't complain that you are too busy, and more importantly, don't say you believe the concepts are worthless. When and if an initiative comes your way, embrace it. Tell your supervisor you will be happy to be trained in the concepts. When you are asked to implement the new concepts, be ready to show everyone how you have implemented the new program. Remember, there is far more risk to being in the camp of doom and gloom, than in be in the camp of cheerful believers.

> *Several years ago I was working in a large organization that learned about Six Sigma. This was an initiative that transformed Motorola and General Electric and saved money, as reported by their executives. My organization hired a group of high priced executives to manage the program. The first thing they did was to hire an expensive consulting firm and contracted with them to design and deliver a training program. Now this consulting firm had no experience with Six Sigma, but that was not an obstacle. My supervisor came to me and asked me to become involved. I stood at attention and asked, "Where do I sign-up?" Then I recruited 24 people from our organization to become Black Belts. We all went off for many weeks of training, and came back and went to work. Don't ask if we accomplished anything, because that was not important. What was important was I did not buck the system.*

4. CONSULTANTS

Many organizations use consultants to help solve problems. There are many types of consultants who assist firms with projects or have specific expertise that may not be available within the organization. Most consultants are very helpful and will add value. Consultants who are brought into the organization to transform how business is conducted may fall into the category as potentially dangerous to your career. Typically, you will not be asked your opinion about the use of a particular consultant unless you are in the upper echelons of the organization. It's important to understand that consultants have to deliver a product—and that product often is to recommend changes. Your goal is to be on the positive side of any change.

Business change consultants may not be any smarter than the people in your organization. Their solutions often are not solutions developed by a world-renowned expert in a particular field of study. They often glean solutions from within your organization. Consultants typically will repackage existing concepts and sell them as their own ideas. The typical consulting process includes these steps:

- Fact-finding or diagnosis. The consultant expends billable hours interviewing people.
- Analysis. Analysis is implemented using Microsoft Access or other data management and data manipulation tools.
- Data display. Consultants are artists when it comes to presenting the data. It will look sexy.

- Idea generation. The consultant picks the brains of the people within the organization and then uses presentation skills to package the results.
- Solution selection. Good consultants will attempt to steer the customer's personnel into a solution of the business problem they were hired to fix. Then they will claim the solution was co-developed mainly by the customer, not the consultant. The consultant will simply state he or she provided facilitator skills. This may sound confusing, but consultants know they have to give credit to people who may hire them again and again. Therefore, they will try hard not to antagonize the organization's personnel. Also, by giving credit to others, they will spread the risk of blame if the solution fails to deliver the expected results.
- Solution testing. This is where the real smoke and mirrors act comes to the stage. Because the consultant only tests the solution at one point in time and he or she often controls all aspects of the testing, the outcome almost always is successful. The consultant wants the customer to sign-off on the completion of the project, so he or she can get paid. Therefore the test—if there even is a test—is carefully controlled by the consultant. It would be far better to demand a series of tests months after the consultant leaves the premises.

- Reporting recommendations. In a big meeting, the consultant provides a sophisticated presentation to upper management.
- Selling additional services. A good consultant never leaves a client before he or she has identified another area that can be improved by using the services of the consulting house. The consultant often will provide a low estimate of costs that will sound enticing to the management team.
- Leaving. A consultant will leave the premises fast as possible, before people start to poke holes in the results of the study.
- Invoicing. This will come minutes after the consultant leaves your property.

The consultants may interview you or ask you to produce reports, data, or records. During this interview, the consultant is looking for solutions to the assigned problem and for other problems the organization may be experiencing. When the consultant interviews you:

- Do not forecast doom and gloom. This is not the time to complain about terrible work processes because your think your supervisors are dumb and do not listen to the workers. Consultants often will not hesitate to report back

to their project sponsor about the people who complain about the current management. The consultants have nothing to lose, but you certainly could lose your job.
- Do not complain about other people's performance.
- Do not describe how you would change the way organization is run, if only you were given the chance.
- Be honest and don't withhold data.

When the interview is over, take the time to document your discussion: What data was given? What hints did the consultant give you concerning future recommendations? Don't be afraid to discuss this with your supervisor. This is considered a "cover-your-ass" maneuver that might be necessary later. Remember, the consultant will package all of the findings and deliver the "developed" solution, which is the product they expect to sell to management, and then deliver an invoice. In the event you are asked later why you discussed or recommended a specific point, you will be able to present your minutes of the discussion. If there is a question by management of your statements, that could lead to a question of your loyalty or capability, you will at least have some objective evidence to counter the argument.

5. BUSINESS TRAVEL AND ENTERTAINING

During my career, I traveled all over the world. Many of these trips were to suppliers, customers, or other of my employer's organizations. Traveling often was a significant part of my position. But, business travel is not glamorous. Most of the time you travel alone, fly or drive to a location, check into a hotel, conduct the intended business for the day, and then return to a hotel. In between, you typically find some place to eat your meals, and you often are alone except when you are expected to entertain the customers or people you are visiting.

Expenses

When you spend the company's money, you often have to submit an expense account. Review the company's policy about obtaining receipts and make sure you know which receipts have to be submitted with your expense accounts.

Rule # 14 Never live off an expense account.

Attempting to cheat the company is completely unacceptable.

Think about the real costs of cheating on a single expense account. Depending on company policy and the need for receipts, you might be able to get away with an extra $100. If *you were making $50,000/year, and then get caught and fired, do you think cheating to get an extra $100 would have been a good decision?*

You should be able to produce a receipt to support or explain every expense you charge to the company. Never charge off a personal expense to your company. Before you incur any expenses, find out if the company will issue credit cards or provide cash advances. If you are issued a credit card, get a copy of the rules for using the card. Remember, this is a company card, not a personal card. Complete your expense account as soon as you are back in the office.

Travel

Learning how to survive while traveling is often described as trial by fire. Talk to your fellow co-workers about the tricks of the trade: Which airports should you avoid? What should you do if an airport like Chicago O'Hare shuts down while you are waiting to fly out? What you should not say to airline personnel? Good luck, it can be fun on the road. Here are some tips I can pass along:

- When you are required to go on a trip, use the company's authorized method for booking reservations. If the company requires you to use a specified travel company, don't bother trying to get a better rate using the Internet.

Surviving Your Career

- One of the most important travel skills you will need is to learn how to wait. When traveling by air, you are required to get to a terminal early—and then you wait for a flight. Many flights today are connecting flights, and in between flights—you wait. Flights can be delayed—and again—you wait. While you wait, hopefully you'll read, listen to music, or if you have a laptop with a wireless connection, you'll work. Don't get into the habit of waiting in an airport bar. That can only lead to trouble.
- Believe it or not, airport airlines personnel will assist you as long as you are courteous and patient. Remember to say please and thank you.

I have been in Chicago O'Hare more than once when the entire airport was shut down due to weather or computer problems. In situations like these, thousands of people's flights have to be cancelled and rebooked. Remember patience. I remember being in lines for hours waiting to talk to a frazzled ticket agent. I saw people yelling, cursing, crying and even threatening these poor airport personnel. I even saw ticket agents call for police to come to protect them because they believed they were in danger from an irate customer. When it was finally my turn I displayed empathy for the agent and apologized that they had to be involved with this situation. I respectfully asked for any possible help with rebooking an-

other flight. I never asked for extra consideration for a meal or a hotel. Because I was patient and respectful, I often was provided with a flight the next day and often was upgraded to first class. I also was given meal and hotel vouchers. I always thanked the agent profusely, and then sent a note to the airlines commending that employee.

Lodging

If you are responsible for choosing lodging on your trip, do not select the most expensive hotel with the best restaurant or swimming pool. Instead, choose a hotel that is convenient to the location where you have to work or attend a meeting. If the closest hotel is very expensive, review this choice with your supervisor first before you book your reservation.

Dining

You can get a good steak dinner for $25.00: You do not have to eat in a 5-star restaurant that serves the same steak for $50. Many organizations authorize a maximum amount of money you may charge to your expense account in one day (per diem). If you spend over this amount, you will have to cover that extra expense yourself. You can't charge it back to the company. If you travel with your supervisor, follow his or her lead in selecting restaurants. Then, allow your supervisor to pick up the tab.

I was once traveling in Japan with my boss and he decided it was our turn to pay for our dinner and that of our Japanese hosts. Our hosts were the President and staff of an organization from which we wanted to license technology. Therefore, they were suppliers. We went to a restaurant that our hosts selected. As usual, we all had drinks and many courses to our meal. The dinner lasted for hours and finally, it was time for the check. In Japan at that time, it was not courteous to settle the bill in front of your guests. My boss told me to go to the restaurant's front desk and give them my credit card. I nearly fainted when I looked at the bill! There were eight people in our party. The total bill, including a service fee, was the U.S. equivalent of $2500.00. I slowly signed the bill hoping my boss would not have trouble approving my expense account when I returned to the United States.

Before you leave on your first trip, discuss the company's policy for drinking alcohol with your supervisor. If there is no policy, do not charge a huge bar bill to the company. Use your head and drink in moderation, if at all. Do not drive if you have been drinking alcohol. An arrest for a DUI while on company business will end your career. Your company will not cover any costs associated with a violation. In addition, your organization will not tolerate any improper behavior as a result of drunkenness, especially in front of customers and suppliers. Remember you are representing the company and any problem behavior on your part reflects poorly on the organization as a whole.

<u>Entertaining</u>

Discuss the company's policy for entertaining during company business, such as taking customers, suppliers, or other company personnel to dinner, shows, sporting events, golfing, or many other forms of entertainment that I'm too sensitive to mention. Understand the limits, because there often are ethical and legal rules that apply. One example of both an ethical and a legal issue is offering a bribe. If you are trying to obtain a contract from the customer, would taking a customer on a golfing holiday be considered bribery or simple entertaining? If your company performs work for the Government, you will find it is illegal even to offer to pay for a meal. The Federal procurement regulation considers this type of entertainment as bribery.

6. COMPANY SOCIAL EVENTS

Many organizations have holiday parties, gatherings to celebrate business successes, or outings combined with a meeting to communicate strategic and tactical plans, etc. Whatever the circumstances, these events put you into a social setting with people from many organizational levels of the business where you are on public display away from the business arena. It is perfectly OK to enjoy yourself at these events, but always remember it is essentially still a business environment.

Before you attend a company social event, determine the proper dress code. Use good taste and consider the purpose of the gathering when selecting your clothing. It will be a social and career mistake to arrive at a large dinner event dressed in shorts and a tee shirt when everyone else is wearing ties, jackets, or stylish dresses.

Many employers avoid serving free alcoholic beverages at company functions. This prevents potential legal issues if an employee who gets drunk at a company function and is involved in an auto accident after leaving the function. Therefore, if booze is not offered free but is available for sale, watch how much you drink. In fact, it would be best not to drink alcohol at all. Remember alcohol will also loosen your tongue. If it is free and everyone is imbibing, drink less than you would normally. Better yet, "play the game." Fill up a glass with water, tonic, or ginger ale and walk around with it.

Even at a social event, your conduct will be noticed. This is not the place to play practical jokes, show off on the dance floor, attempt a seduction, or get into an argument with a co-worker. Others will see and remember your inappropriate behavior. This also is a situation where you should be careful about the topics you discuss with others. (See the section on "Trusting co-workers.") This is not the place to challenge anyone in management by describing a process for improving profitability or service to customers. If someone asks a question, answer it, but watch what you say. Don't commit to doing something simply to make an impression: You will be held accountable for completing the task. Don't openly criticize anyone or the operation of the business, even if you believe the criticism is well deserved. A social scene is not the time or place to have these conversations.

There may be events where you are asked to bring a partner. Make an effort to introduce your partner to co-workers and your supervisor. If your partner may have trouble remembering people's names, try to help out during the event when you run into people again. In the event there have been situations where either you or your partner has had affairs with other co-workers or co-workers partners, it might be best to avoid the event altogether. The last thing you need is to expose emotional wounds or unleash an open display of hostility.

7. COMPANY SPORTS TEAMS

Playing on a company-sponsored sports team is an excellent networking and team-building opportunity and also is a good way to demonstrate your interest in the organization. Conversely, if you're not athletically inclined or simply don't enjoy sports, there is typically no downside if you chose not to participate. As in "Company Social Events," watch how you behave and what you say during a match. Remember the warnings about drinking alcoholic beverages.

As you know, some sports such as basketball, hockey, and even baseball involve physical contact. And while playing sports is great physical activity, there always is always chance you could get hurt. Think about the sporting activity you want to play, and ask yourself, "Could I get hurt?" Then, think about your specific job and consider what would happen if you could not use one of your hands or lost your ability to walk as a result of a sports injury. You might be faced with living on Workers Compensation wages, instead of your usual wage. Can you afford to do that? The other consideration is health insurance. Will your current insurance fully cover the costs to treat the injuries, and at what deductible? And co-pay?

My son ended up needing surgery on his ankle after hurting himself on a climbing expedition. It took him months to recover, and he was not able to perform fully in his job. Because his medical insurance coverage was inadequate, Dad picked up the bill!

It is okay to be competitive, but don't endanger another player simply to win a point, especially if you are competing against another team from your own organization. Remember, getting hurt at a company-sponsored event may result in a lost-time accident. Then Workers Compensation will kick in, which will cost your organization big bucks. So play to win, but not to hurt anyone.

C. TENDING YOUR CAREER
1. YOUR RESUME

As soon as you arrive on a new job, update your resume. Have it ready for immediate distribution. A new job may only last a few short days or weeks.

> **Rule # 15 Your resume must always be up to-date.**

> **Rule # 16 Your resume shall not contain any false information.**

In recent years, it has become increasing easy to verify a person's past employment. There are businesses that offer services to employers that verify a job applicant's education degrees and positions with previous companies.

Because downsizing is so common in today's business world, an employer usually will understand if there is a gap in your employment history. Always be honest about the reason these gaps exist.

Many job applicants stretch accomplishments or even overstate the number of people they once supervised. Most of this is difficult to verify because past employers often will not discuss any details beyond the dates of employment. Do not exaggerate your capabilities to get hired for a new job for which you ultimately will not be qualified. If you really only had 10 people in your organization and you effectively managed the group, do not insert one more zero and make it 100. You just might not be capable of making the leap to an organization of that size. This creates a career disaster.

2. TRAINING

If you think you have the necessary skills to perform your job and can impress those around you with your knowledge—think again—you probably can learn more. You have to earn the right to be trained. But the company typically will not flood you with training offers unless it is in its best interest or you have been hired into a training assignment.

Internal training

Soon after you arrive on your new job, determine if your organization offers internal training, and if so, review a list of course offerings. Develop a wish list of courses that interest you. Hold onto this list for future use and update it from time to time. During performance reviews with your supervisor, it's OK to ask if you can attend a selected course, but be ready to defend why it is important to you—and how it will benefit the organization.

If your company does not provide internal training or does not have a formal list of offered training opportunities, be prepared to identify your specific training needs. You may be able to identify subject matter experts within your organization. If the need is critical, find out how you could obtain the training from those people. Remember, you have to earn the right to be offered the training.

> **Rule # 17 Remember that training costs money.**

Product training

All organizations offer a product, and it is important to learn the specifics of the product, regardless of your position in the organization. Find out if your organization offers product training. Learn the "lingo" about the product. Then when someone in a meeting refers to the "green slip widget," you'll dazzle everyone by discussing the product using the proper terminology.

Self-training

Self-training involves learning as much as you can about how your organization conducts business. Begin by learning who is involved with different aspects of the business so you will know where to turn when you are asked to perform a task. Make it a habit to ask people what they do in the organization and to describe the major process steps for their area of responsibility. Make mental notes about the sequences all of the processes from start to finish, as well as who is involved with each step. Once you have an adequate handle on these people and processes, your productivity will improve. Your supervisor also will notice you have the ability to absorb business discussions and ask relevant questions with ease.

Advanced degrees

Working toward an undergraduate or advanced degree is a serious, expensive, and time-consuming step. However, your interest in pursuing an advanced degree may fall into the categories of either "nice to have" or "required by my profession." If a degree is not required for your current position, you have to assess how a degree will help your career.

Consider these examples:

- Suppose you are a mechanical engineer for a large manufacturer of equipment. You have been on the job three years, directly from undergraduate school, and you think a MBA would be nice to pursue. Your company has a tuition reimbursement benefit, but will not allow you to take time off to pursue the program. In this case you would have to do the entire program after working hours and it would take four years.
- Perhaps you like working as an engineer and want to remain in the engineering field. You particularly like research projects designing and building new products. Would having an MBA help with this career path? No. Therefore, do not pursue an MBA. It might be better to go for an advanced degree in engineering.

- What if you are beginning to see that the engineering field is limited and you want to move into a management job somewhere else in your organization, even operations or marketing? In this case, an MBA might be useful.
- Say you are a skilled mechanic and you have the ability to fix equipment. You like what you do and realize that you probably would not like an office environment. Your salary is OK, but you realize that some point it will reach an ultimate level. Your company offers tuition reimbursement, but only for subjects related to your job. Both your wife and your best friend think you should go back to school and finish your undergraduate degree in forestry management. While it may be nice to have a degree in forestry, it will be expensive and may or may not help you fulfill your career ambitions.

Once you think a degree <u>might</u> be useful, you still have to determine if it's worth the time and money to pursue it. It may be helpful to do a reality check:

- Talk to co-workers in your organization who have obtained a degree. Ask a specific question: What has the degree done for your career?
- Talk to a Human Resources staff member: If a managerial position were open, would only people with degrees be

considered, or would weight be given to experience and accomplishments?

- If you belong to a professional society, ask a sample of other members the same questions. You might continue your benchmarking study by selectively contacting headhunters. Because they sell people to organizations, they probably will be able to offer helpful advice on this issue.
- If a degree is required for your profession, will your organization pay the tuition and allow you the time to pursue it? Many organizations will agree to pay for tuition using Federal Income Tax Guidelines but will require you to remain with the company for a prescribed period of time after reimbursement—a relationship often referred to as "the golden handcuffs." In this case, you won't be able to leave the company right after getting your degree.
- Can you pursue a degree part-time? Most degree programs require a significant amount of work, including researching, reading, writing reports, or making presentations. Classes typically are held once or twice a week for two to three hours per course. When you already are committed to your normal workday and your responsibilities at home and then add classroom hours and your homework, you will be putting in long and exhausting

days. You are the only one who will know if part-time studies are realistic for you.

Again, compare your expectations with those people who already are in the program you would like to pursue. Find out how they are balancing work, school, and their personal lives. If you believe you can overcome all of these challenges and have a burning desire to obtain the degree, then go for it!

3. PROFESSIONAL SOCIETIES AND CERTIFICATIONS

Many career fields have professional societies. Check on the Web to determine if appropriate societies exist for your field—then join. A professional association will benefit your career by providing opportunities to:

- Network with peers
- Benchmark ideas and processes
- Access potential job opportunities
- Participate in continuing education
- Work toward professional certifications
- Teach subjects to your peers about your particular specialty. Teaching is always an opportunity to learn, gain exposure, add to your resume, and produce networking opportunities.

Some professional societies require members to pay dues, and your organization may cover this expense. Regardless of whether you receive reimbursement, there is value in joining if you make the effort to be involved. Attend meetings, lectures, training sessions, conventions, write articles for the society's magazine, and seize the opportunity to offer training and lectures on your area of expertise. All of these will take on added value when you are either looking for a new job or are out of work. During my career, networking contacts from a professional society were useful in helping me find new positions.

I was working as a Quality Control Manager and became acquainted with a college professor at a university. We met because my chapter of a professional society used his academic department to teach a course on Quality Engineering. During my participation in the course, I made a point of having several discussions with this professor. After the course, we kept in contact with each other. Then one day he called and asked me to help him because he was on the board of an organization that accredited organizations providing auditing services. He called me because he knew I was very active in the professional society. That contact led to an opportunity to make money as an independent contractor over the next six years.

Professional certifications come in two general categories:

- Certifications such as for nursing and physician licensing, hairdressing, firefighting, etc., are often administered by local, state, and federal agencies.
- Peer-recognition certifications such as the American Society Quality, Certified Quality Engineer, and many others.

Is it worthwhile to become certified? You bet! For one thing, it looks great on your resume. Here's an example of an actual job listing for a Quality Assurance Manager:

> *The ideal candidate will have at least 5 years of Quality Engineering experience in a manufacturing environment with a significant degree of involvement with aerospace and defense-related business activity. This position requires a B.S. degree in an engineering, mathematics, or science discipline. This individual must have demonstrated skills in statistical process control and conventional quality control and problem solving techniques. The candidate must have experience with implementation and administration of ISO 9001:2000 standards. CQE, CQA, or CQM* is highly desirable.*
>
> ** CQE, CQA and CQM are peer recognition certifications offered by the American Society Quality and carry tremendous weight within the Quality profession.*

Often the certification requires that you participate in continuing education, which will help make sure you stay current with innovations, trends, ideas, and technologies within your field. Continuing education programs also provide networking opportunities, all of which are important for career survival.

4. PERFORMANCE EVALUATIONS

Organizations have different ways of evaluating their employees. Some processes are formal and others may simply be informal discussions between the employee and the supervisor. In any case, it is important for you to prepare for your evaluation. Regardless of how you believe your performance has been since the last evaluation, keep in mind these realities associated with performance reviews:

- Supervisors often have difficulty writing a performance review. It's easy to give a positive review, but it is very difficult developing the correct wording for a negative review. It is even more difficult to deliver a poor performance review to the employee. Therefore many supervisors simply avoid the subject by never stepping up the bar and delivering an honest message.
- Once the review is written, everyone involved typically forgets it. In my experience, most reviews have been treated as a bureaucratic requirement. Once the manager

and the employee have completed the necessary steps to create and sign-off the document, it is filed away and never looked at again. Often there is very little follow-up.

- In the case of a review for an employee who is not meeting the performance expectations of the position, regardless of whether the supervisor had the courage to "tell-it-like-is," the employee is doomed to be fired or never given an opportunity to get a promotion. The supervisor will take any opportunity to remove such an employee from the organization either by firing the person or, if the supervisor is unethical, allowing the employee to accept another job in a different department.
- Typically, compensation changes are not connected to the performance review. In many organizations, raises are determined once per year during a budgeting process. It's possible that even when you receive a great performance review, the raise you finally receive may be mediocre.
- You can expect to be asked to evaluate yourself against the goals you and your supervisor agreed to the previous year. Hopefully, you will have kept a running history of your achievements and will be able to document your accomplishments. If you have not met the goals, be prepared to document the counter-measure(s) you are

implementing to attain them. Admitting failure without having a recovery plan is tantamount to surrender. It is not a good tactic for career survival.

- You probably will be asked to identify steps necessary to further develop your future with the company. This means the organization is allowing you to request training or to name a different position that will enable you to further your professional experience. Do not be bashful, but keep the request for development steps within reason. If you state that you think it would benefit the organization to send you to Harvard Business School for two full-time years, don't be surprised when your supervisor laughs in your face.

Now, depending on your age, you may opt to decline to identify development steps. Recognizing this is often a sign to management you have decided that enough is enough, and that ending your career is in your future plans.

Most performance reviews put you in front of your supervisor to discuss your review. Again, many supervisors are uncomfortable with this chore, so be ready to help out with the conversation. Have a script ready of the points you want to discuss. If you want to discuss a problem, make certain you can offer a possible solution. Recognize co-workers who have helped you achieve success, but be careful of making achieve success, but be careful of making accusations of people who may have contributed to any failure. This would only demonstrate your inability to find solutions and work effectively with people in the organization.

5. COMPENSATION AND HOW TO GET MORE OF IT

Compensation is based upon the laws of supply and demand.

Suppose there are 10 organizations in your geographic area that need 20 experienced mechanical designers. If there are only 5 available people looking for a new job, then the laws of supply and demand will kick in and those 5 people will be very sought after. There might even be a bidding war for the 5 designers and the offered pay will rise. If the organization cannot afford to offer this raise in pay, it will not be able to recruit qualified people and eventually their business may suffer.

Positions and pay ranges

Many organizations have established compensation schemes based on a given quantity of levels and a range within each level.

For example, let's assume your position is a Level 7, and you are currently making $55,000 a year. The pay range for a Level 7 is from $44,600 to $69,800, with a mid-point of

$57,200. In other words, your actual pay is below the mid-point for Level 7. If you are performing spectacularly, you could present a case to your supervisor to bring you up to the mid-point. This would be a $2,200 raise, or 4 percent: Not bad, as most raises in the United States for the early part of the 21st century are averaging 3 percent or less. Your manager could probably give you the 4 percent and not seriously endanger other increases for people in the organization.

Remember, most managers typically are given a set amount of money to distribute. Their supply of money for salary increases is not unlimited.

Let's assume you went to see the boss and demanded a 10 percent raise, which would set your compensation at $60,500. Now you are above mid-point and you have used up $5,500 of money available to your boss for all raises. Unless you walk on water or are able to blackmail the supervisor, it is unlikely you will get this raise because the manager needs some of the $5,500 to give to other deserving co-workers.

> **Rule # 18 Aim for a promotion rather than a raise—but you have to earn it.**

In many organizations, you could get a large raise as a result of a promotion, along with the potential of a higher salary in the future. Therefore, a better strategy is to move to a new level and get more money as a result of a promotion. Moving to a Level 8, with a new range of from $49,100 to $76,700 and a mid-point of $62,900 is a new ballgame.

The other alternatives include:

- Getting a new job with an organization in a geographic area where there is a labor shortage in your profession. Even in 2006, there were labor shortages for certain skills within the United States. Machinists could almost name their pay because the supply of competent machinists was very low. The same holds true of pharmacists. Do your homework, but be prepared to move. (See section on "Moving.")
- Putting your name on the "street" in your own geographic region, which means seeking employment but not having to physically relocate. Sometimes just changing jobs will result in a good raise, but there are other considerations. (See section on "When is it time to leave")

CHAPTER IV. CONSIDERING CHANGE
A. WITHIN YOUR CURRENT ORGANIZATION

1. MOVING TO ANOTHER CITY

If you are thinking about moving, hopefully it is because of a good career opportunity with additional compensation, either with your current organization or in a new organization. But making this decision and then being happy with the outcome depends in large part on whether you are single and unattached, single and working on an attachment, married and want to stay married, attached and want to stay attached, or finally the big one—have children. (Hopefully there are no other choices!) Let's just assume you have worked out the decision to move with your partner and there are no complications. I know from experience, if you get past that hurdle, you have accomplished a lot! However, there are additional factors to consider:

- Cost of living. If the price of real estate at the new location is twice as much for your house, do a cash flow analysis or review your family budgeting needs using your new salary. It might not be worth it if you are only getting a 10 percent pay increase.
  Suppose your current home is valued at $150,000, you have a $75,000 mortgage at 6.0 percent for 30 years, you have lived in the home for 5 years and your payment for

principal and interest is $450 per month. Let's assume you can sell your house for $175,000 and walk away with $85,000 for a down payment on a new house, and the same style house in your new prospective location costs $300,000. This leaves you with a potential mortgage of $215,000 at 6.0 percent, or $1289 per month. The incremental difference for monthly payments is 286 percent, not 10 percent.

- Family income. If you depend on your life partner's income to survive financially, determine how long you can survive if that person doesn't find work quickly at the new location. If he or she stays behind until a job prospect develops, you may have to support two residences for a while.
- Property ownership. If you own property, can you sell the property in a reasonable time period? The real estate market is fickle, and what you believe to be a certainty may never occur. Have a back-up plan. Do the math and determine if you be able to maintain two residences along with utilities, etc. Calculate if you will be able to afford to rent an apartment at your new location for a period of time. Your new organization may offer to cover these costs for some period of time, but this point has to be

negotiated before you accept the position. When you do your planning, be pessimistic and plan for an extended period of time, such as 18 months.

- Family separation issues. If you have to leave your partner behind until you sell your property, what are your plans for returning to visit? How often will you travel? How long will it take to make the trip? How much will it cost? What effect will your absence have on your family during the time in between visits? If there are children, the parent who stays with the children often will be under tremendous stress in the absence of the other parent. The children will be affected as well, and very young children often will act out by behaving badly. This behavior often is their way of saying that they miss you.
- Children. Moving probably will mean the children will have to go to new schools. This is a significant transition for children of any age. If you are fortunate, your move will take you to a community with a good school system, but this might not happen if you have not done your homework. When you are on a house-hunting trip and have selected a potential geographic area, take the time to visit the schools to talk to an administrator. If your children are in elementary school, plan on having a discussion with middle school personnel as well. In addition, take the time

to determine if there are private schools in the area, and if so, visit them to discuss why parents are sending their children to a private school rather than a pubic school. In addition, your children will be leaving friends and trying to make new friends. During this period, expect less than stellar behavior from them as they struggle to adapt. This may tax your patience, but be forgiving: After all, you are the one who decided to move for your career. You can help ease this transition by spending more quality time with the family and helping them get acquainted with their new community.

- Financial strains. Don't be shy about asking questions when you are negotiating your compensation for your new position. Will your organization provide financial assistance with relocation costs? The costs for selling and buying a house are not insignificant. Then there also are costs for moving your belongings, temporary living arrangements, meals and lodging in transit, as well as income tax implications. The difference in the cost of auto insurance from one state to another may be a shock. For example, even though New York State has high taxes, auto insurance is reasonable. Then look at insurance rates in Kentucky or West Virginia—out of sight!

- Social issues. If you grew up in the eastern part of the U.S. and are considering moving to an area such as rural Indiana, for example, have you considered the cultural differences between the two locales? Yes, religious issues should be taken very seriously. Let's assume you are Jewish or Hindu and you have a desire to practice your religion by going to services and having social relationships with people who also practice your religion. Will you be happy in rural Indiana if the Jewish or Hindu population is almost non-existent and there isn't a temple in which to practice your religion? What if you have to move from a coastal locale to a region that is relatively landlocked? Would this geographic difference affect you? Most people don't care about this either way, but others may long for the personal comfort they experienced when they lived close to the ocean. Finding social connections in a new locale may not be easy, depending on your age and whether or not you have children. If you have children, it's easier to make friends with people of your own age group. If you are older or do not have children, this social transition may be more difficult.
- Your new community. Think about all of the tasks you will have to manage when you move: finding new doctors, dentists, hair salons, pizza and bagel shops; arranging for

change of address for all normal correspondence; finding a new supermarket; learning a city's road system; and getting a new drivers license and auto registration if you are changing states.

After you have considered these factors associated with moving for a career change, you'll be in a better position to make an informed decision about whether the move is good for your career, your family, and for you personally. Just remember, if you make a bad move you probably will recover, but it may be expensive. If you have never moved to a new area, be prepared for a lot of extra work. Even if you have professional movers, the moving process will demand a significant amount of your time. Therefore, make certain your new employer understands that you will need the flexibility to meet with a realtor, search for housing, make arrangements for purchasing and selling a house, etc. The transition process often takes several months. Be prepared for an adventure.

2. TAKING A JOB OUTSIDE THE UNITED STATES

Seize the opportunity to broaden your skills with a job outside the United States. Today, having global experience can be a phenomenal boost for your resume and future, as long as you are successful in the offshore position. There are several issues to consider before you accept a job outside the U.S.

- Where is the position located?
- Is it safe to live and work there?

Take the time to research the location in order to determine if it is safe for your family. For example, there were many job opportunities with U.S. firms in Iraq in 2006/2007 —not very safe! The same is true for many locations that are not in a state of war. Mexico is not involved with a war, but kidnapping of foreign nationals is a thriving business. If you found a great job in Mexico City, you may be surprised to know that you will need to hire a bodyguard to escort your children to a private school. While your children are in school, it may be advisable to have the same bodyguard take your wife to the beauty salon.

If you doubt the safety of a proposed location, don't leave the United States. An excerpt from the U.S. State Department's Web site related to personal safety in Mexico warns at a point in time:

"Kidnapping, including the kidnapping of non-Mexicans continues at alarming rates. So-called express kidnappings, an attempt to get quick cash in exchange for the release of an individual, have occurred in almost all the large cities in Mexico and appear to target not only the wealthy, but also the middle class. U.S. businesses with offices in Mexico or concerned U.S. citizens may contact the U.S. Embassy or any U.S. consulate to discuss precautions they should take."

Family considerations

If you feel the new location would be safe and you want to take your family with you, find out about schools and how the women in the family will be treated. In many countries women are treated as second-class citizens and do not have many civil or legal rights.

Health risks

Health risks such as water quality (poses risks of water-borne illnesses such as dysentery or the famous Montezuma's revenge), air quality (may threaten those with respiratory problems or allergies), and the quality and availability of health care will affect your decision to live in a foreign country. The U.S. State Department's Web site, www.state.gov/travel, is an excellent starting point for research. There are companies in the U.S. that specialize in preparing people to travel overseas. One such company is Passport Health®, www.passporthealthusa.com. Another alternative is to have a discussion with your family physician.

Cost of living

In most places in the world, Americans find the cost of living is higher than in the U.S. for a similar lifestyle. Real estate here at home is inexpensive compared to London, Paris, or Hong Kong, for example. Therefore, it is important to determine how your employer will compensate you for any disparities in the cost of living.

Compensation and taxes

Negotiate with your employer how will you be paid, and whether you will be subject to taxes in both the U.S. and the country where you are working.

Communication issues

Accepting a position in a foreign country where you do not speak the language may not actually benefit your career. However, if you really want to accept the position, have your organization fund your enrollment in language classes so you can learn the language as quickly as possible.

Social, cultural, and legal aspects

Laws, customs, and cultural norms vary greatly from country to country, so it's important to familiarize yourself (and your family) with these aspects in your host country before you arrive. Before leaving for your new posting, research the social customs and laws of the country. Do not become an "Ugly American"—first impressions last with new acquaintances. And, breaking the law in a foreign country may become the worst nightmare of your life.

Coming home

Keep in mind that if you were successful while you worked abroad, it's unrealistic to think you'll get your old job back. First, your position probably will have been filled while you were away, then again, hopefully you will have grown past that position. If your current organization is not willing to use the skills you learned while working abroad, look for a new organization that recognizes the value of this experience. We are in a global economic environment today, and many organizations will be happy to hire people who have worked outside the U.S.

3. YOUR FAMILY'S IMPACT ON YOUR CAREER

For the purposes of this discussion, let's assume you are either married or have a significant other, and both you and your partner have immediate families. It's important to maintain a balance between the efforts you devote towards your career and to your family. Of course, if you are the principle wage earner for the family, then receiving your wages on a scheduled basis is important. But is it necessary to spend 80+ hours per week working to sustain the wage? Any tension created at home also will eventually begin to show at work. Poor performance as a result of family problems is not a valid excuse with any organization. There is no one answer, but family turmoil can be demoralizing and divorce is not inexpensive.

Changing jobs and possibly moving to a new location can be relatively uncomplicated if you are not married or attached to a significant other. However, you may still need to consider your immediate family, such as parents or siblings. If you can justify the move, issues may arise as your parents' age and require more assistance. If you are 1000 miles away, it will be hard to respond with assistance when they call you. Now, how can that affect your career? At some point you may have to leave work, fly home, and deal with the crisis. This could affect your career (and your wallet) if it happens too often.

You also may need to convince your spouse or partner to leave his or her family behind when you change jobs. This is a very tough issue to face, especially if your in-laws are elderly and your significant other is very close to them. You might have to pass up a career-enhancing opportunity because it simply does not work for the family.

The same is true if there are children involved. Some people say it is difficult to move a child who is in high school, but realistically, there is never a good time to move with children who are attached to their friends and their community. All I can say is that children tend to be resilient. They probably will be very upset with the prospect of moving, but most children manage to work through the issues and survive with your help and understanding.

But wait! What happens it the tables are turned and your working spouse or partner comes to you and says he or she has a career opportunity in a different state. Do you give up your job for your spouse? Can you stay on your career path by following your partner? There are several alternatives:

- Legally separate or divorce. Extremely expensive, and if there are children involved, not a wise move for either of you.
- Stay at your current position, but move when you find a comparable position located near your partner. This may be the best alternative, but if it extends into a long period, could produce problems at home and at work.
- See if your significant other can negotiate a position for you with the same organization. Move to that position, re-establish your presence at the new geographic location, and if necessary, look for a better position after a short period of time. Yes, you will face the job-hopper tag, but it will be defendable.
- Investigate a parallel organization. If you are currently working for a large company, find out if there is a branch or affiliate of the company where your partner's new job is

located. If there is, find out if you can transfer to that business location.

- The virtual office. Another alternative, depending on your current position and the dynamics of your current organization, is to work from your virtual office. This means you can perform all of your duties via computer and telephone. Today, using both methods allows meetings to be conducted with participants from around the world. You can display presentations via Web meeting software and verbally communicate through a conference call. Your paycheck probably will be direct deposited into your account. Will you be allowed to keep your current position but work from home in a different location? If you don't bring up the possibility, you will never know if it is an option.
- Live separately. This usually is not an acceptable option for the long-term unless you have a creative relationship.

4. EXPLORING OTHER OPTIONS

What if you have reached a point in your career where you might be considering a change in careers but you do not want to change organizations? As an example, let's look at a typical career change—from a Design Engineering department to Sales. If you are relatively young and there are still plenty of years before your retirement, a career change could be feasible, but bear in mind that there are risks associated with leaving your comfort zone. The term "relatively young" has to be interpreted to mean the number of years left in your working career where there is room to recover from a mistake.

> *I had started my career working as a Quality professional, and thought I had found my niche. While I was working at a large organization ($250 million sales per year), I was offered a detour into Production Control. I was still in my 30s when I took this turn. This change was a drastic mistake on my part—simply a bad fit—and ultimately forced me to leave the organization. I ran back to the Quality field and remained there until I retired.*

Before you have a discussion with anyone about changing positions, take the time to do an inventory of your personal assets or skills that would ensure your success in the new field. Write these down, along with specific education, skills training, or other development tools you will need. You'll need the time and funding for any required education that may only be available outside of the organization. Be ready to estimate the time and cost necessary to make the switch.

If you still think changing careers makes sense when you have completed your analysis, it's time to discuss the concept with people in the organization. The first person you might want to talk to is your rabbi. (See Section: Choosing your rabbi.) If you have chosen this person carefully, it should be easy to bring up this subject. Ask your rabbi to be objective and try to poke holes in your argument about changing careers. Depending on the outcome of this discussion, you might want to have a similar discussion with a person outside your organization whom you respect and who is more experienced than you are.

Once both your rabbi and your outside contact have given you their blessing to proceed, it's time to talk to someone within the organization who has some level of authority. For example, if you want to move into Sales, make an appointment with the Sales Manager. If you receive positive vibes from this discussion, have a discussion with your own supervisor. In fact, you should assure your supervisor that you don't intend to leave your job until a position in Sales is available and your old job is filled. Do your best to make your supervisor feel comfortable, but recognize that from this point forward, your supervisor may treat you differently. But that's OK. Remember, you plan on leaving anyway.

The next step is to work with the Human Resources department to begin the plan. (Unless the Sales Manager can create a new position for you, you will have to wait until a position opens up.) Expect to get an entry-level position and expect to have to learn new concepts. This definitely is starting over, but at least it was your choice. What happens if you go down this path and realize after a while that you have made a mistake? This could happen and you'll need to plan on leaving the organization to restart your old career unless you have obtained a "get-out-of-jail" card from your former supervisor before leaving your old position. The actual chances of this happening are rare, unless there just happens to be an open position in the organization with the appropriate pay grade to match your current one.

5. TEMPORARY ASSIGNMENTS

There may be a temporary opening to fill when someone in your organization leaves or is promoted. To accomplish the work left behind, someone from management may approach you to assume these new duties temporarily. What should you do? Management frequently is desperate to fill a temporary void because these vacancies frequently occur without notice and business needs to continue. The good news is that someone may think enough of you to seek you out.

Now you have several immediate questions to ask when you are offered such an opportunity:

- Define temporary? How long will this situation last?

- Will you be expected to perform the new duties in addition to your current responsibilities? If so, how will your performance be measured—you already have a full-time job? There are only so many hours in a day, and managing too many additional tasks often results in marginal performance.
- If the temporary position is considered a higher-level position, will your compensation change?
- Would your employer consider formally hiring you for the new job and then immediately hiring someone else for your old job? This would be a beneficial deal, assuming the new position is attractive to your career. Remember, you still will need to manage both until your old job is filled.

> **Rule # 19 Do not turn down a temporary assignment before you have explored all of the alternatives and potential consequences.**

If you think it would be valuable to stay with your organization and are seeking a promotion, accepting a temporary position is a good idea. Let's also assume you have obtained satisfactory answers to the questions above and you are ready to start your new duties. Here are several thoughts to carry with you.

- You still have to take care of your old duties.
- Treat the new assignment just like a new job. Learn the responsibilities and processes associated with the new assignment.
- Look and learn before you begin to implement changes. Even if you have prior knowledge of how the previous employee managed the job, do not plan to make changes until you fully understand all of the implications and have reviewed the potential changes with your new manager.
- If you are asked to be a supervisor, abandon any prior bias you may have had about the individuals on your team. Take the time to win their support. You do not want to waltz in and quickly gain a reputation as a dragon slayer. If indeed you find there are bad apples in the crowd, follow the proper procedures for managing personnel who are unproductive or ineffective.
- As soon as it's practical, develop a game plan of supportable objectives. Then meet with your supervisor to achieve consensus.

B. THINKING ABOUT LEAVING

1. WHEN IS IT TIME TO LEAVE?

Considering leaving an organization for any reason is a serious prospect. It certainly is not a decision that should be made in anger. Any job change is essentially a gamble because you really cannot predict how things will turn out. You may think you are leaving an unacceptable position, but you may land in different organization with an unbearable environment. Remember when you were interviewing to join your current organization? How much did you really know about the cultural environment and organizational dynamics after the interviewing process? How often did the environment change during your tenure with your current organization? Therefore, jumping to a new organization is inherently risky business, even if you leave for a promotion with more compensation.

Why might you consider leaving?

- You believe you are underpaid and you can get more compensation at another organization.

    Considerations: This is not a good reason for leaving an organization unless you are sure you are terribly underpaid. Look at the section: "Compensation and how to get more of it," and at least ask for a promotion. Remember, if the working environment is great where you are, then moving to a new organization strictly for money may be the wrong decision.

- You are dissatisfied with the way your supervisor treats you.

    Considerations: You first have to decide if you want to try to salvage the situation or go ahead and pursue an employment change (or a combination of both). First ask yourself: Is this a short-term issue or has it gone on for a long time? If it has been a short-term issue and your supervisor is approachable, request an opportunity to have a frank discussion. A face-to-face conversation may produce a solution. In fact, you may learn the problem is not with your supervisor, but rather with your performance. However, if you have a supervisor who has a history of being a "900 hundred pound gorilla type," then this could be a risky approach. If the problem is harassment, unethical requests, or you feel you have been treated unfairly compared to your co-workers, then you might want to consult with the Human Resources department. Yes, there is some risk with this path, but what do you have to lose? If they fire you, you could threaten to take legal action against the company. (Most companies shy away from litigation.) If the situation has been going on for a long time and you have made attempts to rectify it through established avenues, then the choice is yours.

- You do not see any potential for advancement within your current organization.

    Considerations: If you already have applied for several jobs within your organization that are a step above your current position but were not selected for any of those positions. Ask the hiring supervisor why you weren't hired. The reason you weren't selected may be legitimate, but correctable. If you can solve the riddle of why you were not selected, then do some work determining the likelihood of being hired for other open positions within your organization. Think about the positions you believe would be your next step. (Hopefully, there will be more than one.) If you can determine the age of the people in those positions and how long they have been in their jobs, then you can estimate the likelihood of their leaving that position.

    If a worker is 52 years old has been in a position for 3 years, is doing a reasonably good job, and is not likely to move anytime soon, then it's unlikely that position will be opening anytime soon. In this case, it's probably an appropriate time for you to leave. But, if you think there are other potential positions opening within an acceptable time period, then reassess the situation. Why start looking for other jobs?

- You want to switch career paths and you can't do it within the current organization.

    Considerations: This one is easy. If you have the skills and/or training for a different career path and your current organization does not need someone with those skills and training, then you may as well start your job search.

- You believe your current organization is in financial difficulty.

    Consideration: Don't base your beliefs on this issue on opinions or office gossip: Get the facts. Have you seen a reduction in the level of business? Have there been layoffs? Do you know of customers who have gone to other suppliers? Have some senior executives recently left the organization? These are signals of an organization with problems and your suspicions about the financial health of the company may be well-founded. Now, if your organization is a public company, they are required to publish financial data. If you do not understand financial reporting, ask a friend who is not in the company to look at the reports and tell you if the data spells trouble. This trouble may include an operating income loss over several reporting periods, an increase in short-term debt, or an increase in accounts payable. Then, if you are convinced the organization is in trouble, it's probably time to start looking for a new job.

- You have friends working for another organization and they say it is a great place to work.

    Considerations: Frankly, this would be a dumb reason for leaving a secure position and moving. Forget about it!

- You are bored with your current position and do not foresee doing anything to change the situation.

    Considerations: First re-read section "Bored-looking-busy." If nothing works, you don't foresee any change, and you cannot hide—then it is time to leave.

- Everything about your current job has been OK, but a headhunter has contacted you with an apparent amazing opportunity.

    Considerations: See "Headhunters.

- You have decided to quit working because you have won the lottery, or have inherited a fortune.

    Considerations: Great news, but make certain the amount is enough to live on for many years. Once you take your self out of the workplace you might become obsolete in your field in a very short time. Since you have what you believe is a large amount of money seek professional wealth management assistance before you quit.

- You have decided to withdraw from the workforce. Considerations: This alternative may be an easy choice, depending on your age, physical and financial health, marriage situation, or if you want to stay at home with your children. If you choose to leave, remember that although getting back into the workforce later is not impossible, you might not get back to the previous ending point in terms of responsibility and compensation. Research all of the data regarding your cost of living, savings, and how long your money will last, and then make your decision. Before you leave, do some research about what is happening within your organization. If business is poor, you might be able to negotiate a nice severance package if you volunteer to take a lay-off. This move might also enable you to collect unemployment insurance.

2. JOB-HOPPING

Employers are looking for people who are willing to stay on the job. They want a return on their investment of time to train an effective employee. If you started a job and left within the first 12 to 18 months and then repeated the same pattern with a second job, you would be considered a job-hopper. On the other hand, if you can honestly state that you were on a job for a short period of time and were subsequently laid off due to lack of work, you would not be considered a job-hopper. Job-hopping is a relative term, particularly in the eyes of a potential employer. But, simply put, switching jobs within a short period of time strictly for a lack of compensation isn't a smart move.

Even if you are bright and have significant talents to offer the organization, it's important to understand that there are still many things for you to learn, and compensation only comes to those who pay their dues. Yet, you say, "I have an engineering degree from MIT." Your credentials don't mean anything until you learn how to apply your degree to products or services offered by your employer. How long that will take varies: Your employer will think it takes longer than 18 months.

All of this does not mean you should stay in a bad situation if you have only been on the job a short time. If you consider yourself capable but find yourself in a losing situation with your supervisor, then it is time to get out—but be ready to be labeled a job-hopper.

3. ARE YOU THE OLDEST PERSON LEFT IN YOUR ORGANIZATION?

What if you arrive at work one day and suddenly realize you are the oldest person in the organization or work group? It could mean you have long-standing value to the organization and they have not tried to push you out the door. Today, there are three types of organizations:

- Organizations that value the knowledge and skills of older workers and therefore nurtures these people. These organizations reward their employees' contributions with appropriate compensation and recognition. They understand it is difficult to replace experience, even if a younger employee will generally accept less compensation. Although you may have started thinking about retirement, think again—you are valued.
- Organizations that believe older employees are "coasting" and therefore should gradually be put into less important positions. (This attitude is based on the unfounded belief older people cannot keep up with the pace of business.) These organizations recognize that it is illegal to attempt to force older workers out, but they use other techniques to make them feel uncomfortable.

What if you have been given a "special" assignment to study the possibility of moving a product line to another location because someone in management thinks it is a good idea? An assignment like this probably has no value and probably never will be seen by a decision maker, but is intended to keep you busy and out of the way. This type of organization probably hopes that older employees will tire of this treatment and leave on their own. If you think your organization uses these techniques, do not leave unless it happens to you. Then, if you can keep from getting too bored, work a plan to force them to attempt to fire you. The plan is simple: remain at your position as long as you can stand it. Perform any task that comes across your workstation, but if there is no work, make it obvious you are between tasks. Someone will wake up eventually and probably make you an offer to leave because it will be obvious you are really only a part-time employee. When this happens you can negotiate a great severance package.

- Organizations that simply want to clear the decks of older workers, believing they just cost too much to maintain. These organizations may offer an early retirement package, but many organizations are doing away with retirement plans anyway. They may have layoffs or temporarily eliminate positions. What if it just so happens that one of those positions is yours? If you think this is happening, find a lawyer to take your case and threaten legal action—but hope you do not have to sue. All you want is to get a sweeter severance package because the organization has already decided you are no longer useful.

4. HOW TO QUIT

> **Rule # 20 Do not burn bridges.**

If the reason for leaving is emotional due to mistreatment of any kind, do not have any emotional outbursts with either co-workers or supervisors. Once you have made the decision to leave, for whatever reason, take care of the following:

- Personal items. You should already have cleared your workspace of most of your personal belongings, except for the items that are normally visible to others. Leaving the organization is strictly a private decision and it should be an absolute surprise to all co-workers. Starting to carry out all of your personal items before you give notice will send a signal you may not want to convey. Do it carefully or wait until you give notice.

- Give notice. There is nothing mandatory about giving a two-week notice, but this falls under the category of not burning your bridges. Plan on allowing for a two-week notice, but if you have already lined up another job, have an arrangement where you can start immediately if need be. You may find your current organization asks you to leave immediately after you give notice anyway. In fact they may walk you to the door and send you your personal items later. If you have any personal data stored on your office computer, delete the files prior to giving notice. Your organization will most likely demand you leave the premises immediately if you are moving to a competitor.
- Write a letter of resignation. Simply state you are leaving the organization to pursue another position, effective immediately. You do not have to state where you are going, nor name the position. Offer a two-week notice. Say thank you, and sign the letter. Give it to your supervisor and do not get involved with a long conversation. Wait for your supervisor to ask any questions and answer them honestly, but without any emotion. If you are asked where you are going, only give the name, if the new organization has authorized you to name it. It is acceptable to say: "I rather not give you the name yet, because all of the details have not been completed." At that point, be ready to

be escorted out of the building. If you are escorted out of the building after giving notice, some co-workers may contact you later to gossip. Again, be careful of what you discuss concerning why you are leaving and where you are going because you may again come in contact with old co-workers or supervisors who may be in a position to influence your future.

- Health benefits. Assuming you have a new job, be certain about the health benefit coverage start date. Typically, coverage from your old organization may last to the end of the month in which you have resigned, but it's always better to be sure about these assumptions.
- Other benefits. Ask to talk to a Human Resources staff member about ending your benefits such as insurance coverage, retirement benefits, 401K plan transfer, unpaid vacation, and your last paycheck. Make certain you know the name of the person to contact for this information. You probably will be able to conduct this business by telephone or schedule an appointment to discuss your questions.
- Exit interview. Many organizations want employees who resign to have an exit interview. This process helps the organization understand why you are leaving and how improvements can be made to avoid losing more people.

Again, during this interview do not burn bridges. If you are leaving for additional compensation, say so. If it is because your supervisor was a miserable SOB, be polite and make up something to say such as you are leaving to pursue new opportunities in a learning environment. Most organizations will not fire a supervisor because a single employee said he was a miserable so-and-so!

5. GOSH, I WAS FIRED OR LAID OFF

When you are fired or laid off, more often or not, this may come as a surprise to you. You might have even heard rumors of layoffs, but deep down, you hoped it would affect someone else.

Firing results from your poor performance or some grievous act on your part. On the other hand, a layoff typically is the result of your company's poor financial situation where they can no longer afford to pay you. The difference between the two is how your organization treats you after giving you notice. Well, what if your day arrives and you have to deal with these situations?

- If you are fired, do not expect to be treated well. You may not receive any severance pay. There is no legal requirement to pay severance unless you have a written contract, or if there is no language in the contract discussing "dismissal with cause." You probably will be asked to leave the premises immediately without returning to your desk. The organization may allow you to return to your desk to pick up your personal items, but you can be sure that someone will be watching you. Do not expect anyone from this company to give you a decent reference of any kind. Finally, most of your co-workers probably will treat you as a pariah. You will be history.

- If you are laid off, you probably will be treated more congenially. Your organization may give you a few weeks notice. The layoff may not be effective immediately and if you can find another job within the organization during that time, you will be able to stay, but at a new salary. If you are asked to leave, you probably will receive a severance package depending on your tenure with the organization. You probably will not be walked out the door immediately and you will be allowed to return to your work area to pack up your personal items. Depending on your past performance you will be able to get positive recommendations. The organization may even offer outplacement services. If these services are offered, take advantage of them. Your co-workers who survive the round of lay offs eventually may forget you, but they probably will have some degree of empathy while you are going though it.

<u>Recovering</u>

Once you are out the door, regardless of whether you were fired or laid off, go home and sit down. It's common to be emotional and angry with yourself, your old boss, your co-workers, and the old organization. You should not be driving around aimlessly or visiting a bar. Just go home and calm down. Do nothing until the next day. This will give you an opportunity to reflect and start the planning process with a clear head. Once you have arrived at a place where you are no longer angry or tearful, start the recovery process. There are several phases in the recovery process:

- Financial considerations. Your primary source of income will either have already stopped, or will stop at the end of the severance period. Hunker down and plan to survive. Immediately apply for unemployment compensation. Create a budget and plan for a significant reduction in spending for discretionary items.
- Planning a job search. Regardless of whether you were fired or laid off, do an autopsy: What happened? Why were you let go? You need to come to terms with this because you will need to be able to explain the reasons

when you seek employment. The answer to these questions also will help you plan a direction for the new job. (Reread the section on "Your resume.") Decide where you want to look and determine the type of job you want. Write down the pros and cons for each decision, and at the end of the day, develop objectives for the actions you will need to take the next day. Then determine how you will proceed to meet those goals. Obviously, the Internet is a great tool. It will allow you to see many potential opportunities, but do not expect that all organizations list all positions. Therefore, you might need help from agencies, headhunters, or your network of friends and business acquaintances.

- Executing a job search. Once you have developed a plan, start your job search. Looking for a job is hard work, so plan to attack the search like a normal day at work, and spend at least 8 to 10 hours a day working on the search. Keep records of e-mails, telephone contacts, names of organizations, and what was discussed during telephone calls. Send e-mails to thank the people who have networked with you for information, leads, or other assistance. This will help people remember you. If you are pursuing an Engineering Manager's position at Company X, maintain a record of all correspondence, e-mails, and telephone calls for the specific position. The records will allow you to research what was said or communicated when the need arises. Follow up on possible leads, but do not make a nuisance of yourself. The hiring manager does not need the annoyance of excessive telephone calls or e-mails asking about the status of the hiring process. Remember, the hiring process is difficult, often requiring the hiring manager to step away from his or her normal duties to work the hiring process.

- Obtaining a job offer. Just get the job offer and get on with it.

> **Rule # 21 If you do not ask, you will never get it. The "it" is money, a new position, a promotion, etc.**

6. HEADHUNTERS

If you need a job, a headhunter can help you find one. If an organization has a position to fill, a headhunter can find the right person to fill it. Some organizations use their own networks to identify candidates, but there still are some organizations that use headhunters to help fill selected positions. Some people would argue that the day of using headhunters is over because it's so easy to find open positions and job opportunities on the Internet. But many organizations do not post jobs on

Internet sites: They actively seek out candidates for their open positions.

Many headhunters will offer to find a candidate to fill a position, but will agree to be paid a fee only if their candidate is hired. Other headhunters are hired as exclusive agents on retainer by an organization that wants to fill positions. Just remember, headhunters have to be paid by someone.

If you need a job, headhunters will be interested in you for one of two reasons:

- They are working on a search for a particular position and your background fits the bill. Then it is a matter of luck and timing if you happen to contact a specific headhunter exactly when you need a job and he or she just happens to have a corresponding position to fill. It pays to stay in contact with headhunters because they might be searching for someone with your qualifications.
- Headhunters often specialize in certain fields and like to have a stable of people who might be interested in changing jobs if the right opportunity arises. In this case, even if you are not looking to change, it's a good idea to send your resume to a headhunter to keep on file in the event a good opportunity develops for you.

Headhunters who have been retained to fill specific positions are the best detectives and body snatchers in the world. They burrow into an organization without knowing who is available and come up with names of people who might be interested in open positions. They just keep digging until they find likely individuals—then they present those people to potential employers to fulfill the search. Therefore, when you get a call from a headhunter, it will be in your best interest to respond. You may or may not be interested in the position you are offered. But if you are not interested in the particular offering, the headhunter will always ask if you know someone who might be interested. Provide a name, even if you do not know if that person is totally committed to changing jobs. Headhunters remember people who help them, and someday you just might need the assistance of one. In other words—one hand washes the other.

7. NETWORKING

Networking can be a valuable tool if you need a job or are looking to change your present position. It's a good idea to maintain a comprehensive list of people you can contact if you find yourself searching for a new position. These may be people you have worked with in the past, met at professional society meetings, while attending seminars, or are personal friends, and friends of friends. If you have no friends and have been working solitary in a deep cave, forget about networking.

> *A friend of mine lost his job suddenly without really understanding why it happened. It actually was the first time this person had ever been asked to leave a position, and it really "rattled his cage." His immediate reaction was to keep it secret from people he knew because he was ashamed of the situation. When I learn about his situation, I advised him to totally reverse this strategy—to tell everyone he knew or met! In other words, network!*

If you are out of work and networking, encourage those with whom you are networking to discuss your status with others. In fact, you want them to discuss your status with others because it could lead to further valuable networking. However, if you are still just thinking about changing jobs, be careful with whom you network. Tell your contacts up front that you are still currently employed and they should check with you before they discuss your job status with anyone else.

C. OTHER OPTIONS
1. SHOULD YOU MARRY THE BOSS'S OFFSPRING?

This one is easy. When in doubt—don't do it—unless you have already proven to the boss that you can add significant value to the organization. If you have not won the boss over as an ally, marrying into the family may make your life on the job miserable.

> *Let's play with this situation. Suppose that after working in the organization for 14 months, you became involved with the boss's daughter while she was a summer intern. You have had no real contact with the boss because you were down several levels in a mid-sized organization. Once you became serious with the young woman, she brought you home to meet the parents and the boss learned for the first time that you worked in his organization. This is not the end of the world, but he soon puts you under a microscope. He sends the word via organizational lines to "watch this kid who is interested in my daughter." Soon, life as you knew it changed: either because people in the organization thought you were protected, or the boss didn't know you and was really trying to make it rough. If you had been closer to the boss and had developed a relationship based upon your accomplishments **before** you became involved with his daughter, your situation probably would have been quite different.*

You also should realize that if a relationship like this does not work out, you probably would be fired, unless the boss and his spouse love you more than their own offspring. Now, if the boss owns the company and is unhealthy, marrying the boss's offspring has opportunities, since you might find yourself running the company if your father in-law passes away. I will leave all of the possibilities to your imagination.

2. WORKING IN A FAMILY-OWNED BUSINESS

Family-owned businesses come in all sizes, and many are very successful. As an example of a huge family owned business:

> *Wegmans Food Markets Inc. is a family-owned retail grocery store giant, based in Rochester, NY. Their sales are in the billions and Wegmans often has been recognized by several professional publications as the best companies in the United States to work for.*

There are several issues here that could affect your career:

- Family ties. Many owners tend to have relatives in the business, whether they are capable or not. It is important to know who these people are and how they are related to the principle owner—daughter, son, brother-in-law, etc. Their rank in this chain often equates to the amount of influence they have with the owner. If you understand the relationship, you may be able to avoid a disaster when working or talking casually with one of the relatives.
- Let's face facts. If you and one of the relatives are being considered for the same position in a promotion, the

chances are you will lose. This assumes the relative is somewhat capable—but perhaps not as qualified or experienced as you are. Too bad! Relatives will win unless the owner is truly an enlightened individual. Your best bet is to plot a career path within the organization that does not conflict with one of the relatives. If you cannot see your way around this scenario, you'll have to consider the alternative of leaving and re-starting your career with another organization.

- What about the heirs? What if the owner is getting on in years and there are no family heirs? In this case, do not be surprised at the chaos if the owner should die suddenly. What if there is a will and the business is left to a distant relative, the surviving spouse, or a charity—but none of these parties are interested in running the business? Then there will be a management void until the heirs sell the business. What would you do? Ask yourself if you are in a position to buy the business and run it. If not, could a group of employees execute the purchase and operate the business? All these alternatives should be discussed with interested employees prior to the death of the owner, and possibly directly with the owner. If there is no possibility of a buy-out due to the size of the business, be prepared for significant change in business-as-usual once the business is sold to a new owner. The new owner may decide to bring in a new management team, move the business, or implement drastic cost cutting. Any of these scenarios might affect your position.

3. STARTING YOUR OWN BUSINESS

Have you ever thought that you might like being your own boss? Thousands of people go this route and many are successful. But, how about a reality check:

- Many people who attempt business ownership and fail often end up in deep financial trouble. If you need to re-enter the job market to restart your cash flow, don't be overeager to accept the first job offer. Rushing to accept a job in desperation without fully evaluating the opportunity may solve your financial problems, but may result in a poor career choice. This would be very similar to marrying a new partner within a month or two of getting a divorce. Although it might be hard to delay taking the right job, take the time to fully investigate all potential opportunities.
- Suppose your business does not make it financially and you have to start over working for someone else. Should you list a failed business on your resume? If your venture lasted at least a year, you should list it because it is not wise to leave significant gaps in the chronology of your

resume. This leaves an opening for others to wonder where you were during the gap. Were you in jail? Did you have a health issue? Just report, "Self-Employed Business Owner," and mention the scope of the business. Of course, questions will come up during an interview, so be prepared to be honest.

- Taking time out to attempt a business venture will affect your career path if the business activity was not associated with your previous career field. For example, if you left your position as a software designer to run your own window treatment shop for a year or two, you might find that software technology had passed you by in the interim. Therefore, be prepared for your career to take a "hit" if you attempt to return to work for an employer. On the other hand, if the economy turns a corner and you find your career specialty in hot demand when you return to the workforce, then you would be immediately employable and your career progress would not be affected.

4. HOLDING A SECOND JOB OR MOONLIGHTING

Everyone's financial situation is different and the reasons for having a second job may be the difference between survival and debtor's prison—or you may simply want to build wealth. If you are planning to take on a second job, first assess how a second job will affect your primary position and consider these questions:

- Does your current organization have a policy about employees holding down a second job?
- Will the second job conflict with normal working hours?
- What will happen if your supervisor asks you to work extra hours with the primary job?
- How will you handle the fatigue factor?
- Does your second employer compete with your primary employer? If so, don't even think about taking the second job.

You will need to inform your supervisor that you are thinking about taking a second job. Be honest about why you are taking a second job. If it is because you are desperate for money, you might be pleasantly surprised if the supervisor offers you more money for your current job. It's a long shot, but you never know!

If you are planning to run a business in addition to your regular job, good luck. Some people do this and are successful. There are several additional considerations:

- Your business cannot complete or conflict with your employer's business. If you have any questions concerning a potential conflict, discuss it with your supervisor. Be honest. Don't use the same suppliers. For example, don't try

to arrange a bargain from the same advertising company by leveraging the business from your employer.
- Do not conduct your business during the working hours of your primary job. If you think this is not possible, it's time to decide where your loyalty lies.
- Remember, many people attempt to run small businesses on the side but fail for many reasons. Do not burn your bridges with your current employer—you may need that job!

CHAPTER V CONCLUSION

A. MANAGING SUCCESS AND SURVIVAL

Determining if your career has been successful often is easier than you think. Success doesn't necessarily have to mean you have become a millionaire or the president of a Fortune 500 company. It could mean you have arrived in that place in time where you are comfortable with what you have accomplished and can confidently say you are satisfied. You probably have been able to secure your financial future, in spite of all of the uncertainties of medical costs, pensions, Social Security, and health and safety of your family.

How will you know when have arrived at that mystical point? Well, you'll just know.

> **Rule # 22 Be honest with yourself.**

You will be able to look back and reflect on the work you performed, and how your co-workers perceived you, how you treated other people, and if you were able to balance your career with your family life. If you believe you were successful, then you will have passed along your experiences to others and, by doing so, helped and influenced them, and taught them some of what you have learned along the way. Finally, success will mean you will be in a position to simply say good-bye to your career—and leave.

We all proceed down different paths and encounter both joy and hardship along the way. We hope the many choices and decisions we face during our careers will lead us toward success. Of course, one book cannot cover every issue that could possibly affect your career. However the issues explored in this book represent the challenges I personally faced during my career. In fact, as this book was being written, I was the oldest person in my organization; I accepted a somewhat temporary assignment; I grew bored with my position; I grew tired of the bureaucracy within my company, and I decided to leave on my own terms.

Nevertheless, I am proud of my career accomplishments. Yes, I made a few unwise decisions along the way, but when I reflect on my career as a whole, it was not too bad.

My son, who at 28 was starting his career path, asked me a question concerning my impending retirement. He asked me: "Do you think you made a difference during your career?" I had to think about an answer for a while, and then said that I may not have made a financial difference within any of the organizations I had worked. They were mostly large companies, and though I knew my chosen trade, my successes may not have been financially visible. I then said that my legacy would be the people who worked for me, and with those people who implemented the many quality systems I designed.

As I moved through my career and grew older and wiser, I had the opportunity to work with talented people who were generally younger than I was. Whenever possible, I mentored them, assisted them with challenging positions, and encouraged them to seek advanced degrees. I was not simply the boss who won on all ties, but someone who took an interest in, and in some cases, helped several co-workers with serious personal issues such as terminally ill family members. I was proud to be able to make a difference in the lives of these people.

Whenever I was asked to work with a group of people to design a quality system, I made a point of understanding the human side of the business. Organizations are made up of people first, and when you are asked to design processes and procedures, you tend to affect people's lives. Again, I believe I listened to the human side of business first.

My son went away from this conversation understanding career survival is not simply making lots of money and becoming the boss. It involves being comfortable with what you accomplished during that career.

B. IT'S UP TO YOU

Throughout this book, I have identified 22 Rules. If you remember anything, remember these Rules. As you progress through your career, new events will take place that probably will make some of these rules obsolete and new rules no doubt will be created. That is acceptable—it's your career, and you will have to learn if you have survived or not.

C. THE RULES

1. Come in before your boss and leave after your boss leaves.
2. The boss is always right.
3. Use sick or personal days only when absolutely necessary.
4. Do not have sex on company property and avoid having sex with a co-worker, anywhere.
5. Be polite.
6. Never turn your boss away—for any reason.
7. Don't trust your co-workers with your career.
8. The people in the Human Resources department are not your friends. They are charged with protecting the organization.
9. Never turn in a report late.
10. Do not bore your audience.

11. You are responsible for quality to satisfy the requirements and expectations of your internal and external customers.
12. Never hesitate to report a substandard product.
13. Embrace new programs with enthusiasm.
14. Never live off an expense account.
15. Your resume must always be up to date.
16. Your resume shall not contain any false information.
17. Training costs money.
18. Aim for a promotion rather than a raise—but you have to earn it.
19. Do not turn down a temporary assignment before you have explored all of the alternatives and potential consequences.
20. Do not burn bridges.
21. If you do not ask, you will never get it. The "it" is money, a new position, a promotion, etc.
22. Be honest with yourself.

Made in the USA
Lexington, KY
05 March 2011